WIN
WIN

WIN WIN

HOW TO CREATE MUTUALLY BENEFICIAL RELATIONSHIPS THAT GROW YOUR BUSINESS

Laura Meyer

WIN-WIN: How to Create Relationships that Grow Your Business

Copyright 2022 © Laura Meyer

All information, techniques, ideas and concepts contained within this publication are of the nature of general comment only and are not in any way recommended as individual advice. The intent is to offer a variety of information to provide a wider range of choices now and in the future, recognizing that we all have widely diverse circumstances and viewpoints. Should any reader choose to make use of the information contained herein, this is their decision, and the contributors (and their companies), authors and publishers do not assume any responsibilities whatsoever under any condition or circumstances. It is recommended that the reader obtain their own independent advice.

First Edition 2022

All rights reserved in all media. No part of this book may be used, copied, reproduced, presented, stored, communicated or transmitted in any form by any means without prior written permission, except in the case of brief quotations embodied in critical articles and reviews.

The moral right of Laura Meyer as the author of this work has been asserted by her in accordance with the Copyrights, Designs and Patents Act of 1988.

Published by Happy Self Publishing
www.happyselfpublishing.com
writetous@happyselfpublishing.com

HAPPY
SELF PUBLISHING

DEDICATION

I would like to dedicate this book to the following people:

MY HUSBAND

Mr. John Meyer: The ups and downs we have experienced in entrepreneurship can break marriages apart, but ours has only become stronger through the storms. This book would not have happened without you, and I am beyond grateful. I love you.

MY FAMILY

Andrew, Joshua, and Naomi: May you always learn the value of building long-term relationships, starting with your love for one another. I pray you continue to become one another's best friends and that you'll see this book as an example that anything is possible when you seek to make authentic connections with the people around you. Love you to the moon and back.

YOU

For all of you who are putting yourselves out there every day, doing the hard and brave things, dedicating yourselves to businesses you love, and honoring your entrepreneurial dreams, I salute you. Being an entrepreneur is the hardest thing I have ever done, and it is not for the faint of heart. It is my greatest wish that this book will serve you in ways you never imagined. Thank you for being here.

Download the FREE AUDIOBOOK

To say thanks for purchasing my book, I would like to give you the audiobook version for FREE!

I know that life gets busy and being able to listen to it on the go will give you a better chance of finishing the book. I narrated it myself, so it will feel like I'm right there with you as you have your morning coffee, go for a walk, or ride in the car.

CREATEYOURWINWIN.COM/AUDIO

Video Summary

Want a video summary of this book that will help you start making progress quickly?

Check out this three-step video training and overview of the process.

In this training I cover the following:
1. How to turn your offer into a top of mind, referral superstar.
2. The best strategies to create powerful connections that fuel business growth.
3. The single best way of generating leads and sales without chasing fans, follows, and likes on social media.

CREATEYOURWINWIN.COM/VIDEO

TABLE OF CONTENTS

Introduction *1*

Chapter 1: Networking Is Out, Relationships Are In 9
Chapter 2: A Business Fueled by Relationships 23
Chapter 3: Initiating the Win-Win 49
Chapter 4: Developing the Win-Win 75
Chapter 5: Implementing the Win-Win 101
Chapter 6: Building Community 115
Chapter 7: Don't Fear the Win-Lose 139

Common Questions *149*
Thank you for Reading my book *153*
Acknowledgments *155*
Take Your Business to the Next Level *157*
Ways to Work with Laura *159*
Permissions *161*
Notes *163*
About the Author *167*

INTRODUCTION

"I am so frustrated with social media."

"No one sees my content anymore after the last algorithm change."

"I am at a loss as to how to generate more customers for our company."

"Paid advertising suddenly stopped working for us."

These are the types of comments I hear daily from the brilliant organizations I'm honored to serve as a business growth strategist at JoyBrand Creative, the consulting company I founded that is dedicated to empowering mission-based businesses to accomplish their visions. Trying to grow your business by leveraging digital channels and social media is creating much frustration across all industries.

There was a time when we could create content, and the people around us would magically see it. Doing the simple task of developing good quality thought leadership and distributing it across the internet made our lives easier, streamlining communication and giving us a way to become more productive within the ever-evolving and fast-paced world we live in.

Today, digital platforms have gone from a simple way to distribute information to becoming a place to pay to play. In other words, on most platforms, you need to invest financial resources for other people to engage with more than 5 percent of your marketing. To maximize the visibility of your organic content, you need to know how to keep up with the latest marketing trends, which is difficult at best. The algorithms prioritize different types of content at different times of the year, making it very difficult to keep up when you're also busy running a business, serving your customers, and having a life.

Even worse, as a society, we are experiencing a second pandemic—one of massive disconnection.

In 2018, *Psychology Today* reported that "Researchers have found that people who use multiple social media platforms report more symptoms of anxiety and depression.... Longer or more frequent use of social media also appears to predict depressive symptoms."[1]

On Thrive Global, Thomas Bognanno writes, "When it comes to social media, we often find ourselves comparing our lives, jobs, families, vacations, and bodies to everybody else's perfect posts. Or we get caught up in polarizing politics, letting ourselves get sucked into the latest controversial content. While many of us mindlessly scroll through our feeds to unwind or disconnect from the day, we may be causing more disconnection and dissatisfaction than we realize."[2]

In contrast, when we randomly run into someone that we haven't seen in a while, we may notice that we don't get caught up in comparisons. While we're personally catching up on one another's lives, we're much less likely to nitpick and compare every tiny detail, and in those moments of interaction, we feel less alone. We find common ground and establish real connections in those moments. We learn something new, exchange pleasantries, deepen our connection, and leave the conversation in a better place than when we arrived.

Why is that?

Digital marketing is an incredible tool, and as small business owners, social media platforms enable us to have a broad reach that we could otherwise never achieve. Digital communication helps us to connect with, support, and understand our audience, unlike any other marketing tool. When used correctly, it can be a hugely influential platform.

As an expert in online marketing and a premier consultant to popular online influencers, thought leaders, and some of the country's fastest-growing nonprofits, I have seen firsthand the power of having an enormous audience and brilliant copywriting designed to overcome subconscious objections. We do this work daily with our clients, which is very effective.

But—and this is an important but—if that is *all* we do, there is an impermanence to our approach; it's like building a business on sand. One shake to the system, and it can be destroyed because clicks aren't connections, and audiences aren't relationships.

Living in the ever-changing digital world, we are conditioned to chase popularity or measure a company's success by its follower count, which, in turn, increases our heavy reliance on platforms and the algorithms that drive them. Algorithms and social media themselves aren't the problem; instead, a problem arises when we use social media to replace meaningful relationships.

That's when technology becomes a way to extract what we want from the world, and we stop seeking opportunities for natural reciprocity that are part of human-to-human connection. That's when we disempower ourselves by giving the platforms and algorithms total control over our connections instead of relying on our innate ability to develop influential relationships that drive business growth.

The pandemic has undoubtedly shown us who we are, with a big mirror held up to our humanity. It has magnified whatever issues we had before Covid-19. For many people, isolation and loneliness have become a daily battle. Most, if not all of us, have experienced some form of grief or trauma, and everyone knows someone who experienced significant loss. During those heart-changing moments, it's natural to gravitate to isolation and places that feel safe to us. Yet the time to start rebuilding, creating, and moving forward is

Algorithms & social media themselves

— AREN'T THE PROBLEM —

instead, a problem arises when we use social media

— TO REPLACE —

meaningful relationships.

♡ *Laura Meyer*

now. Now is the time to start rebuilding relationships, trust, and influential connections, increase visibility, and focus on developing an intelligent business and living an intentional life.

When we stop to think about it, relationship marketing is the simplest, most powerful way to increase the most crucial asset in a business—our connections. Relationships, collaborations, and strategic connections are more than nice to have in your business. They're a must-have because *great relationships build great companies*.

Therefore, as you read through this book, I want to invite you to release yourself from feeling like you must chase popularity online to be successful or build the organization of your dreams. Instead, we're going to focus our energy on being extremely well-connected.

Over the last 20 years, I've owned seven different businesses and generated millions of dollars as an entrepreneur. When I look back at my most significant opportunities, major magazine features, fastest years of growth, and key clients that exploded my business, it wasn't social media, viral content, or exchanging business cards that made it happen. It happened through genuine human connection.

So today, at this moment, I want you to imagine ...

... worrying less about creating a magical social media post or viral content designed to grow your business instantly, and instead, imagine having dozens of go-to mutually beneficial relationships that become traffic levers in your business.

... never again having to send out cold outreach or force your offer down the throat of everyone you meet until someone eventually says yes and instead, imagine having a fantastic relationship with your clients and customers, making it fun and exciting for them to refer people to you.

… letting go of the pressure to spend as much time as possible hustling to create an ongoing stream of algorithm-worthy content and instead, imagine developing collaborative relationships with complementary businesses who send you leads aligned with your values and mission.

… never going into another community to force your offer onto others, trying to find someone who will hire you and instead, imagine establishing credibility in the marketplace with a small group of faithful fans.

For so many of us, when we look at the most pivotal moments in our careers, the groundbreaking client or lucky break rarely happens because of viral social content. Having had viral content myself (a LinkedIn slide share with over a million views), I know from experience that it can get you much attention quickly—attention that can die just as quickly.

But when I reflect on what has given me the ability to grow companies and be at the top of my game in multiple categories, I realize it has been the relationships I've developed along the way. Those relationships weren't necessarily a result of attending networking meetings or because I went into those relationships with an agenda. Mutual respect and understanding backed by credibility built up over time gave me opportunities. They opened doors for me—from photographing celebrities to raising hundreds of thousands of dollars of investments to growing multiple companies *quickly*. The formula for growth has *always* been having not just one but different types of mutually beneficial relationships.

Relationship marketing, developing strong and lifelong relationships with your clients, is a lost art that can benefit your business and relationships.

In this book, you'll learn how to build win-win relationships that catapult your business to new heights. I provide a recipe for the art of relationship marketing: how to initiate, discover, create, implement, and navigate lasting business relationships. You'll learn how to develop, step-by-step, the most straightforward marketing strategy on the planet for your business: you show up, get visible, and build strategic collaborations. You consistently demonstrate credibility by creating value for others. Over time, this generates high-end connections.

Relationship marketing is not new, and it's not complicated. It has been around since the inception of business for a simple reason—it works.

Let's do this.

CHAPTER 1

NETWORKING IS OUT, RELATIONSHIPS ARE IN

On May 15th, 2018, I sent a text that changed the trajectory of my life.

I gingerly typed it out on my phone keyboard, trying to find the right words to inform a group of friends that I was closing a business I loved because I had concluded that it was no longer a viable path forward.

It was a devastatingly tricky decision to make because of its impact on my customers, team members, and support system. As a relationship-oriented person, making this decision gutted me. I was walking away from a company I loved building, and from an industry I was passionate about. As I was experiencing this sense of loss, not only related to the company but also related to my own personal identity as a well-recognized figure in the industry, I decided to send a thank-you text to a group of peers—CEOs of other brands—who had given me critical feedback that helped me make this pivotal decision.

After all the support and niceties that went back and forth, each CEO messaged me asking if this would be a good time for me to help them with projects.

One by one, they all came back and asked:

"I've been meaning to ask for your assistance with our customer relationship marketing system. Can you let me know if you think we're on the right track?"

"Our email sequences haven't been performing. Would you, by chance, be willing to look at them for me?"

"We've been struggling with our brand position, and I think it's hurting our sales. Would you be willing to fly out to our headquarters and run a workshop?"

The great consulting company I am proud to own today was born at this moment.

When I was developing the relationships that resulted in these opportunities, it wasn't intentional. These women inspired me, and I did anything I could to create value for them when we were in conversation. Never in a million years did I think that, down the road, they would hire me and jump-start my consulting career faster than I could have ever imagined, especially at one of the darkest times of my career.

This is the power of relationships versus a network.

The truth is that networking is broken. It's common for people to go into networking looking for an immediate return. They're on to the next person or opportunity if they don't see a quick win. When you enter a conversation or community with certain expectations—a sense of entitlement or an agenda in the back of your mind—you'll constantly be scanning for opportunities to score. That's what I often refer to as an extraction mindset.

This is often the premise that traditional networking is built on.

Yet, that's the opposite of how authentic connections are created because real and powerful relationships are rarely developed in the immediacy and urgency of a networking event. They're built over time by proving yourself to be trustworthy and credible while demonstrating authority and expertise.

This kind of credibility resulted in some of the country's top CEOs hiring me to consult for them during the most challenging time in my life as an entrepreneur. Despite my unfortunate circumstances, I had built up enough credibility that my close connections knew that my situation was not representative of my overall capabilities. In the years following, I built a complete consulting client base with a waitlist and launched a popular consulting certification program called Fractional Freedom. This was made possible by a pivotal text to crucial business connections.

THE TRUTH ABOUT NETWORKING

Networking has turned into a spray-and-pray methodology in which the networker seeks to spend as much time as possible in front of as many people as possible to meet clients eventually. But relationship marketing is much more strategic; it's laser-focused on seeking mutually beneficial relationships in which both parties naturally consider how they can reciprocate. Relationship marketing is about giving, whereas networking is often about getting.

Networking has also contributed to a massive amount of noise online. There are many different groups on Facebook and LinkedIn with free networking events, where the game is to be as boisterous and impressive as possible. The most successful individuals in these groups tend to compete to see who puts out the most powerful presence from the moment they appear. You see posts like, "I made 100K last month and bought myself a yellow Ferrari; comment below to learn how I did it." Then there'll be an attractive person in a provocative pose on the hood of an expensive car. Entrepreneurs quickly jump into expensive training programs not only to discover that the aforementioned yellow Ferrari was rented but also that this magic methodology only works for a small percentage of students.

Those of us who aren't naturally the star of the show try to make genuine connections through so-called networking and instead get burned by one-way conversations. As a result, we opt out of all networking activities, longing to form meaningful relationships with those who aren't necessarily the most impressive but show up with the best character.

Yet this is contrary to how we like to operate as humans; we often network this way because we are conditioned to work this way. But when it comes down to it, many of us are wired for reciprocity and authentic connection. It's our human nature. When I see a child on the playground offer to share a snack or a toy with my children, I often see my kids search for something they can offer in return, even if it's a half-eaten bag of chips (sorry, fellow playground mom!). When we're networking, we are often all about our own gain. Still, when we allow ourselves to go deeper with intention, we can see that relationship marketing is about mutually beneficial wins.

Another challenge with networking is that many established entrepreneurs and high-value customers —the kind you would *want* to meet through networking—see it as a waste of time because of being on the receiving end of the aforementioned extraction mentality. And who can blame them? For example, a sophisticated professional may attend a meeting or an event. Still, they'll rarely find someone with whom they can move into an even exchange of information or work on business development initiatives. As a result, the most influential people you'd want to know in your industry or your category often shy away from networking.

As traditional networking is being rejected by so many, the fast-talking, quick-witted, get-in, get-out extraction mindset is being replaced with a deep desire to connect through depth, truth, and intention by instead focusing on relationship marketing. We long to spend less time with people who say all the right things, and we purposely seek out more time with those who are wise. Therefore, in relationship marketing, we look for connections with people who are committed to playing a long game and seek to partner with those who are trustworthy and credible before the ask.

So when we are looking to build relationships, it's common to avoid traditional networking and seek out learning and growth-based environments in which the common understanding creates thoughtful collaborations and connections. Because the truth is that the longer the relationship takes to build, the more likely it is to become mutually beneficial down the road.

For those of you who are marketing to consumers or are nonprofits trying to increase enrollment for your programs, the circumstances may be different, but the principles apply just the same. When we go in too hard and too soon for the sake of efficiency, we forget about the overwhelming amount of noise that so many of the people we serve navigate daily. This noise often shows up in the form of comparison, perfectionism, and not feeling good enough, which can be even more discouraging to an individual who is already in need of help. When we go in instead with the goal being the relationship rather than the sale, we can create value for the communities we serve regardless of whether they enroll in our programs. And while yes, the goal is to grow any organization, when our intention is value first, the companies grow as a result.

The longer the relationship takes to build, the more likely it is to become mutually beneficial down the road.

— Laura Meyer

WHEN TECHNOLOGY FAILS

If networking is broken, what should we do instead? Some might rely on technology or artificial intelligence (AI) to make marketing systems more scalable. For a while, we believed that relationships could be automated, and technology would be a powerful replacement for human interaction through clicks and automated sales funnels. To a certain degree, it was an effective approach. Much like how the dot-com phase came and went in the early 2000s, we started to test how we could automate connections through advances in technology with digital marketing and direct response, and to a degree, it was tremendously successful until it wasn't.

Because of the Covid-19 pandemic, 2020 was a harrowing year for small business owners, including millions of advertisers who were building automated sales funnels, often relying on Facebook ads to scale their offerings. And then... suddenly, it all went wrong. On November 11, 2020, Facebook's AI content-moderation software went hog wild, shutting down a slew of advertising accounts of businesses generating millions of dollars a month, companies with 20 or more people on the payroll, and businesses whose entire existence depended on those ad accounts.

At the time Bloomberg reported, "[M]illions of small business advertisers... have come to rely on Facebook Inc. because the coronavirus has shut down many traditional retail channels. The social media giant has provided new sales opportunities for these entrepreneurs but also exposed them to the company's misfiring content-moderation software, limited options for customer support, and lack of transparency about how to fix problems."[1]

So much for AI replacing human intelligence! To make matters worse, shortly afterward, in Q2 of 2021, Apple boldly announced a new privacy policy that prevented Facebook's advertising tracking code from being fully utilized on Apple devices. Digital marketing insiders called this the "iOS Apocalypse."

From these two events, which took place within six months of one another, we learned that it's important not to give away all our power to unforeseen forces like technology and platforms. While I am personally interested in where AI takes us in the future with certain types of marketing, what we learned from these experiences is that unlike our genuine personal connections, technology, robots, and algorithms don't have a unique and genuine desire to see us succeed as our relationships do. Bye-bye bots.

One thing that we can all agree on is that the world around us is constantly changing. We don't know when technology will disrupt what we're working on, whether Google Ads will prioritize our campaign or whether Facebook will serve our ad to our target customer. When I started a new entrepreneurial career path and texted the group of CEOs, as I mentioned at the beginning of the chapter, I was able to leverage my relationships to create something new. It's helpful to remember that when it's time to pivot—as is inevitably required of us as entrepreneurs—we can't take our Instagram, our ad account, our blog, or our website; sometimes, we can't even take our intellectual property. But we *can* always take our connections to the next version of whatever we create.

The bigger your company gets, the more people you'll have implemented strategies for that put your brand at risk every single day. Yet, suppose you're well-connected and have vital relationships built on mutually beneficial exchanges that fit various needs in your business. In that case, you have the safety net that your business needs to stand the test of time.

The businesses that will continue to thrive in the uncertain post-pandemic landscape of entrepreneurship are the ones that can go back to connections and begin generating leads in new ways through affiliates, customer base, and partnerships. The businesses that will continue to struggle are the ones that don't have those relationships in place or are uncertain how to get started with relationship marketing.

If this resonates with you, but you're starting from scratch, be encouraged! To have a successful company built on relationships, you don't need a high volume of leads, a large following, or a massive list. To be consistently profitable as an entrepreneur leveraging relationship marketing, you don't need to be a social media influencer, keep track of the latest algorithm changes, or pour money into paid advertising. You simply need a core group of connections with whom you can build credibility, increase one another's visibility, and engage in value exchanges.

Kevin Kelly, in his famous essay "1,000 True Fans,"[2] explains that all we need is a group of people who recognize and appreciate our value and can attest to our competence and expertise:

> To be a successful creator, you don't need millions. You don't need millions of dollars or millions of customers, millions of clients or millions of fans. To make a living as a craftsperson, photographer, musician, designer, author, animator, app maker, entrepreneur, or inventor you need only thousands of true fans.
>
> The mathematics of 1,000 true fans is not a binary choice. You don't have to go this route to the exclusion of another. Many creators, including myself, will use direct relations with super fans in addition to mainstream intermediaries. I have been published by several big-time New York publishers. I have self-published. And I have used Kickstarter to publish to my true fans. I chose each format

depending on the content and my aim. But in every case, cultivating my true fans enriches the route I choose.

The takeaway: 1,000 true fans is an alternative path to success other than stardom. Instead of trying to reach the narrow and unlikely peaks of platinum bestseller hits, blockbusters, and celebrity status, you can aim for direct connection with a thousand true fans. On your way, no matter how many fans you actually succeed in gaining, you'll be surrounded not by faddish infatuation, but by genuine and true appreciation. It's a much saner destiny to hope for. And you are much more likely to actually arrive there.

This is why the most successful and influential experts have professional networks and have impact, influence, power, and opportunities through their relationships. If you're building a sustainable organization, you need to know that it's not about the quantity of your connections but the quality.

AMEN TO THE WIN-WIN

When you're getting started building relationships to grow your business, it's helpful to think about your long-term business connections as a beautiful ecosystem that can and will support your business for years to come. This ecosystem is where peers give and receive referrals or introductions, provide valuable insights to each other, and form a community that will stand the test of time. This relationship-based ecosystem is unique; it's a solid and vibrant community in which everyone lifts each other up to serve in their highest capacity and gives the world their brilliance to effect massive transformation and change. Everyone in this community links arms for the common good, and every link in this chain of interest is necessary for the community to flourish.

> A win-win is a mutually beneficial relationship that promotes **THE GROWTH** of everyone involved. When both businesses benefit, it's a Win-Win.
>
> — Laura Meyer

What you're looking for is to continually create an environment where you're regularly engaging with those you've connected with in win-win partnerships. A win-win is a mutually beneficial relationship that promotes the growth of everyone involved, whether it's by increasing visibility in the marketplace, collaborating, being a sounding board, or a referral partner. If it's any or all of these—if both businesses benefit—it's a win-win.

In observing those new to relationship marketing, I find that many struggle with the idea of playing a long-term game in relationship building. That's natural and normal, given the type of world we live in. Business owners often enter into a relationship because they've been told they need to network more or build more referral partners; the networking ends up manifesting itself as a quick shaking of hands while business cards go back and forth, eyes darting around the room seeking opportunities for the taking, all while having quick "What can you do for me?" conversations. The networking ends up in unopened emails landing in the wrong person's inbox or a passive forward with lackluster results. While many of us don't *mean* to have a me-first mindset, that's how it comes across. This "only reach out when you need something" is commonly practiced because of the busy world we live in, but it comes from a flawed perspective. Seeking first to ask from others is counterproductive if you're aiming to build a sustainable relationship-based business. In the upcoming chapters, I'll be breaking down how to create win-win relationships in your business so you can worry less about where your leads will be coming from and pay more attention to how to continually help the incredibly qualified customers you now have the honor to serve.

CHAPTER SUMMARY

As business owners, we're taught that we need to (1) network, and (2) carry out a plethora of technology-based marketing tasks. But traditional networking is broken because too many extraction-minded people are only interested in what they can take. In addition, an overreliance on technology can leave business owners in the lurch if anything goes wrong. Fortunately, there's a better way—building win-win, mutually beneficial relationships that help all parties involved increase their visibility in the marketplace and grow the impact of their organizations.

CHAPTER 2

A BUSINESS FUELED BY RELATIONSHIPS

Twenty years ago, Gino Wickman and Rob Dube met and developed a deep friendship. Each year, they would meet at a coffee shop two or three times for an entire afternoon and talk about life. Rob's life was not optimal; he was stressed, anxious, juggling way too much, exhausted, and on the verge of burnout.

During their conversations, Gino supported Rob by providing an example of an ideal, optimal life. Gino had created The Entrepreneurial Operating System® and was busy building a successful company, EOS Worldwide®, but remained calm, clear, and energized through it all. Rob could feel it exuding from him. Being curious, Rob would ask Gino about the way he was leading his life. Gino would share, and Rob would do his best to incorporate what he heard into his own life.

Rob went on to implement the principles of EOS in his own company, imageOne, as it scaled to multi-eight figures of revenue and became a leading national example of positive workplace culture. After discovering meditation, he wrote a book called *donothing: The most rewarding leadership challenge you will ever take* and began hosting the Leading with Genuine Care Leadership Retreat, rooted in mindfulness and meditation. Rob became a resource to Gino in the area of meditation.

As each of them mastered the disciplines of mindfulness and meditation, their minds were opened to address life's challenges and traumas in a healthy way. They learned how to eliminate fear and ego and lead from a place of love and compassion.

In 2020, they decided to collaborate in teaching others what they'd learned. They developed a company called The 10 Disciplines, and I'm honored to serve them as a growth consultant.

Gino and Rob entered into their new connection thinking, "How can I create value?" and "How can I be helpful and giving to the person in front of me?" The basis for their connection was, "How can I build a meaningful relationship?" Trust grew naturally, and credibility was established. This applies to every interaction when you're looking to create win-win partnerships, whether with potential customers, business partners, or other people in your ecosystem. People can sense your intention to simply come from a place of being helpful, and relationships form without feeling forced. Our energy is totally different when we initiate new connections with a mindset of generosity and helpfulness, and we magnetically attract the right people for our businesses.

There is a common misconception that relationship marketing starts with cold outreach, random messages, or asking directly for a referral. The reality is that the best way to grow visibility for your offer is to first establish credibility before partnering with other experts who have complementary businesses.

Often, networking doesn't work because when we are networking in the traditional sense, we feel like we have to pretend we're someone we're not. The mutual resistance to connection prevalent in conventional networking is a massive barrier to creating relationships that positively impact our businesses. We are so worried about what could go wrong that we often forget the big-picture view of what is possible. The truth is that in industry, long-term growth doesn't start with actions today that give you an immediate return tomorrow. Whether we're running an ad, producing a podcast, or building a sales funnel, there will be significant work involved. As a result of reading this book, you will learn how to develop relationships in the correct way so that your hard work is the *right* work. By engaging in the right work, you can leverage the enormous time spent on marketing more effectively, and as a result find more ease in your business growth journey.

A WINNING FORMULA

While this concept can feel a bit abstract at first, I will break down three easy-to-follow steps to build critical relationships for your organization the right way. When I look at some of the top results my clients have seen from relationship marketing, they all have the same three main components: credibility, visibility, and community.

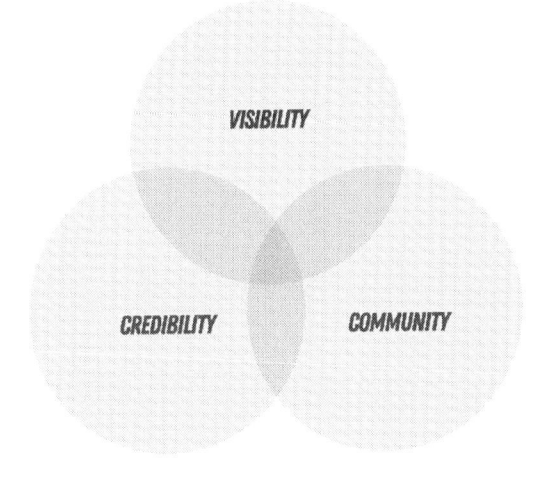

Win-Win
FORMULA

VISIBILITY

CREDIBILITY   COMMUNITY

25

- **Credibility** is the art of establishing trust in the marketplace, which removes people's fear of referring you to others or creating a partnership with you.
- After you have credibility, you want to build **visibility** to stay top of mind with your best-fit partners, clients, and connections.
- With ongoing credibility and visibility comes **community**. When you develop an engaged community or audience for your brand, you leave behind the complicated online noise and open up to the magic of human connection.

While this might feel about as clear as mud at first, in this book, I'll be breaking down each element of this formula and providing you with real-life examples so you can see how it applies to your own business.

Win-Win FORMULA

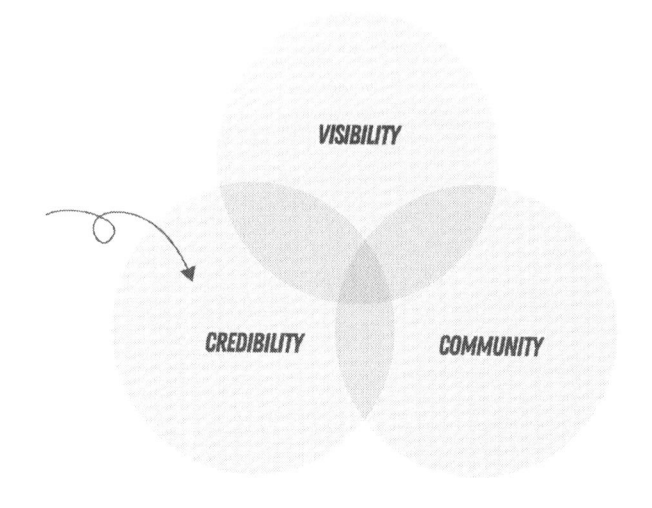

VISIBILITY

CREDIBILITY   COMMUNITY

In subsequent chapters, I'll go into detail on how to utilize all three strategies to ignite the growth of your business, beginning with the art of building marketplace credibility. Credibility primarily begins with developing and establishing a baseline of trust. And yes, you trust the people around you—they think highly of your organization and believe you have a trustworthy mission. But building trust when it comes to relationship marketing goes a bit deeper than your surface-level brand reputation.

WHAT DOES TRUST HAVE TO DO WITH IT?

Dr. Kent Grayson[1,2] runs the Trust Project at the Kellogg School of Management at Northwestern University. He and his colleagues from across the sciences and philosophy came together to discuss the latest research and ideas about how trust works, when it fails us (the heartbreak that can come with broken trust), and what to do when we need to repair it. Most importantly, they looked at how we could quickly establish trust so that others view us as someone they can collaborate with, recommend to others, and call when they are having a bad day. For the most part, researchers like Grayson agree that trust comprises three essential pillars that anyone can quickly implement in their business: competence, honesty, and benevolence.

Competence is the ability to do what we say we can do. This includes proven evidence and specific outcomes from your work. While this is simple conceptually, it's not easy to do. We live in a highly distracted world where so much is expected of us, and our phones often blow up with notifications, zaps, dings, and reminders of everything we forget to do. Consequently, ignoring what isn't essential and staying consistent with what we're committed to is one of the easiest ways to develop trust with others as an expert.

Many of you have demonstrated competence in your organizations. You offer a fantastic product or service and are good at delivering it. Yet there have been times when a client comes to me and wants to start relationship marketing, but they don't yet have proof of concept on that *specific* product line. Suppose you can't yet clearly communicate competence in the marketplace with consistent case students and testimonials related to the offer you're selling. In that case, that will be your first step before engaging in relationship marketing activities. Moving forward before this is in place risks hurting your relationships and is not advisable.

Honesty, or integrity, involves a person or company being truthful—their product does what they say it will do, they don't mislead us, and if they find an issue, they'll acknowledge and correct it. We've all been on the receiving end of a bait and switch, like a late-night infomercial promise that sounded great but ultimately was a waste of hard-earned resources. Honesty is the opposite of that. Honesty and integrity delight us because we live in a world where these traits are often the exception and not the norm.

Honesty is one of those challenging traits to identify because we all like to think of ourselves as genuine people who run honest organizations. I have seen many situations where a program's fulfillment is falling short, and yet the marketing machine marches on. Salespeople continue to push the wrong individuals into a program to meet quotas and hit their numbers. We might unintentionally enroll the wrong people or have unrealistic expectations of those we serve. Red flags often include low participation or completion rate or high cancellation or refund rates for an offering for which I'm serving as a consultant. As leaders, we need to be honest with ourselves when this happens. Back that bus up and fix the programs to ensure we are going about relationship marketing with high integrity.

Benevolence is the surprising unsung hero in building trust. Benevolence is wanting what's best for another person *regardless of how you benefit*. Because so many of us are looking for an immediate win, we need to flip our mindset to embody benevolence in business. We're often set on looking for our next client and operating from a place of scarcity because we start relationship marketing too late in the sales cycle. Benevolence comes from an abundance mindset and is the energy that builds the *most trust* in selling; it's why my potential clients feel taken care of rather than sold on a sales call with me and feel comfortable referring me to their peers. I am candid with an organization if I believe they are not ready for my programs or offerings and will gladly tell them what to do instead. It's the mindset that it's more expensive to bring on the wrong customer or participant than that short-term cash injection is worth.

If you have an abundance mindset, you believe there is plenty out there for everybody, and you'll only make offers to those you're best suited to help. When people recognize that you want the best for them, whether they buy or not, there is a greater chance they will purchase from you in the future. People will enthusiastically refer your company because they know that the referrer is in good hands no matter what happens.

The most challenging paradox in building trust is being willing to grow through relationships while letting go of outcomes. As we pursue organizational growth, we need to become less concerned about whether a relationship will yield a return in the first 90 days and more concerned about creating trust and credibility. A reputation of trust builds relationships and rapport within the communities in which you operate, and as a result, your business will grow over time. Trust is the precursor to credibility, the place from which our business reputation originates. Without trust, we become just another person making claims about why our business is different or better without the street cred to back it up. At best, we just blend in with the noise and become neutral to our ideal customers. At worst, we contradict all marketing efforts because the message we're putting out into the world has no credible foundation.

SOLVING THE TRUST CRISIS

Trust has never been more important in marketing; at the same time, it has never been in shorter supply. Harvard Business Review, in an article titled "3 Ways Marketers Can Earn— and Keep—Customer Trust" reports, "A 2021 survey of 1,000 consumers concluded that more than 80% consider trust a deciding factor in their buying decisions, despite the fact that only 34% trust the brands they use."[3] Business owners looking to grow their companies through relationships need to recognize that establishing credibility is their number one job—not "getting in the right room" or pursuing their audience.

As I like to tell my children when they're acting out at a restaurant, "Read. The. Room." The HBR article states, "You should continually evaluate the effectiveness of your marketing efforts." To evaluate your relationship building efforts, ask yourself these key questions:

- What is my reputation in the marketplace?
- Is my audience engaging with my content?
- Is my following growing or declining?
- Have I followed through on my promises?
- How is my net promoter score (NPS) trending?

HBR concludes, "By regularly checking whether consumers are picking up what you are putting down, you will find that you can more easily meet and even exceed their ever-evolving preferences." Your customer trust will build credibility with potential collaborators, referral partners, and customers.

A business fueled by relationships has three main components: credibility, visibility, & community.

♡

— Laura Meyer

BUILDING CREDIBILITY WITH A NICHE MESSAGE

The second component of credibility is specialization. What many companies don't realize is that they are inadvertently hurting brand credibility with a marketing message that is too generic or general. You may have heard it said that if you speak to everyone, you talk to no one. Successful organizations serve a specific purpose for a clear audience and solve a very focused problem that makes their ideal customer say, "Where have you been?"

Yet so many companies struggle with the idea of clearly articulating the transformation they provide and niching into a clear outcome for their clients. They pride themselves on solving lots of programs for a variety of people, which gives them the feeling that they are effectively living their mission. To help illustrate how credibility relates to clearly articulated outcomes, I want to tell you about one of my consulting clients, whom we'll call Acme Charities. Acme has a legacy brand in the geography they serve, and they do everything from financial assistance to educational programs and onsite childcare. You may know companies like Acme, with tremendous experience in various service lines, which builds their reputation but not in a specific way. When Acme started enrolling more people in a financial literacy program, they had a tremendous amount of value to offer to the people they served. However, they didn't realize that continuing to market the program within the broad umbrella of Acme was holding back enrollments. Acme provided custom solutions to all clients. No matter what the need, Acme was available and ready with a solution.

Soon enough, Acme got discouraged from a low level of high-touch individual enrollment combined with high turnover in the program. They started to feel like the participants weren't interested. Marketing the program was challenging. Rather than feeling fulfilled and excited about financial literacy, I saw how draining it was to the team, with laborious paperwork piling up on the marketing lead's desk.

When I entered the picture, I began as I always do, asking extensive questions about whom they helped and how they helped those individuals.

"Well, sometimes they come in through our other programs, sometimes they meet us at a community table, and sometimes they have issues that keep them enrolling that we help with first," Emily replied. "And if they need a bus pass, we can do that too. And there's another way we can help that doesn't come up often, but if they need it, we can do that too."

The solution was simple but not easy. We rebranded Acme's financial literacy program to a fun-sounding name that separated them from the other offers—a single, simple service that they could deliver to a client to solve a particular stage of their ideal participants' customer journey. This stage is *after* the immediate crisis of not having enough food or proper shelter when the individual has a bit of breathing room to recover from the trauma of being worried about where their next meal will come from. It is only then that we can open up their minds to long-term planning and breaking multi-generational cycles. This made the program more marketable and allowed us to create partnerships with area organizations designed to help those in crisis so that they could not only continue to break the poverty cycle in their communities but also become known as a world-class program for that next stage of intervention.

In the for-profit world, when we niche down, we often find we can charge more than any other service provider because we become specialists and experts in that particular area. In other words, what most organizations need for relationship marketing to work is a more specific business model. After niching down, your network will find it much easier to refer people to you because they know that you will serve that referral with a high level of specificity to that program. This allows many companies to command a higher price and generate steady referrals. They find a niche market position serving a laser-focused purpose with a certain kind of client who needs help with that exact problem.

When your connections know that your service is specific to a particular problem, they'll feel secure in referring people to you. When your connections are experts in other niches, you'll feel confident in guiding people to them. It's genuinely a win-win situation.

The mistake so many companies make is that, like Acme, they have a variety of custom offers that inadvertently hurt their credibility in the marketplace. Some companies I consult for want to help everyone or market multiple offers at once. That can work if you have numerous advertisements or marketing efforts running, each for a different audience. But when it comes to relationship marketing, that kind of marketing hurts credibility. The truth is that you don't have to be the only organization in your industry with your background; you simply must focus on the specific thing you do best. If you're clear on your unique brand, others in your industry become sources of clients instead of competitors. Their businesses don't threaten your offer; they validate it. Why? Because the other experts in your industry offer complementary services that highlight and elevate your marketplace position, and you do the same for them. Even pulling out the service as a stand-alone, branding, and positioning it with a higher level of specificity to a customer segment like I did with Acme Charities can have the same effect. This is why multiple spin-off brands exist within retail and hotel chains. Take the Gap, for example, which sub-brands include Old Navy and Athleta. Of course, it would be much more efficient from an operational perspective for Gap to sell clothing under one brand name. Still, marketing is more effective when it's done with a higher level of specificity to the person it is best suited to serve.

When you're clear and specific about the kind of problem that you solve, you'll find more people who need your help than you can manage. I have seen this time and time again with my clients, which is a great problem to have! I often laugh when I hear clients complaining about how busy they are because of the work we do together. It's what I like to call "good problems" in business. I'd much rather have too many customers than not enough, wouldn't you?

The reason why niching Is particularly powerful in relationship marketing is that the most valuable referral partners you'll find will be people who work within your industry but in a different niche. Having a niche offer also helps make you more confident in what you offer so that you can collaborate with someone who offers something else. Medical professionals, for example, are never afraid of referring patients to each other. A physical therapist will refer you to a podiatrist without worrying about whether the podiatrist will take away their business because both of them are specialists. Being a specialist makes you an obvious choice for a win-win over someone who is a generalist.

Among the different marketing specialists with whom I've had win-win relationships over the years, referral opportunities often arise because they have the expertise, for instance, in a particular customer relationship marketing system. In contrast, as a growth consultant, I'm agnostic to the type of software my clients use. My client might want to implement my peer's technology, making them a fantastic referral. At the same time, my referral partner may have a client who needs a solid big-picture growth strategy, which makes me an obvious referral. If we were both generalists in all things marketing, we would never refer clients to one another; in fact, we would probably be a bit territorial. We would never be able to step into the abundance mindset that comes with the confidence that you specialize in something very specific. But as a specialist, it's easy to recommend or feature someone who solves a different type of problem.

For many companies, niching feels like a four-letter word because they want to help everyone they're capable of working with, and there are a variety of people they could work with and get results. But if your services are too general, the marketplace won't trust you. They don't trust that you can help with a variety of problems and be equally good at all of them because life experience tells them that such broad expertise is extremely rare. For example, when someone gets married, they usually prefer to select their attire from a specialty wedding boutique, not a department store. If you want a specific car you've been saving up for, you visit a specialty dealership, not a general automobile lot. As consumers, we are conditioned to trust experts. By niching, people trust your offer more—they realize that you've helped someone like them and achieved consistent results. Your niche marketing message helps a buyer overcome their fear of losing money and time, a premium buyer's most valuable asset.

Having a niche, a specialty, is the most straightforward pathway to finding others who can refer, collaborate, or partner with your company. The services of a specialized business are referral-friendly because they're an easy ask. They solve a specific problem for a niche person and are easily explained in a relatively short period of time. This makes it easy for people to say, "I know the exact person for you!" to their friends, colleagues, and family members when a problem arises.

For larger organizations looking to generate leads beyond one-to-one referrals, affiliate, speaking, or joint-venture partnerships operate by the same principle. Two more prominent companies with complementary specialties will often partner, reducing customer acquisition costs and leveraging one another's audiences to expand their client bases. By contrast, companies that have large and broad audiences that are fragmented by various offers will not only struggle to increase market share, but they'll also struggle to find growth opportunities through affiliates and partners.

When we get specific about the people we help and how we help them—those we work with and, more importantly, those we don't work with—win-win opportunities open up everywhere. A general business coaching program is unlikely to recommend another general business coaching program unless they're packed with clients. But someone specializing in business coaching that helps multilevel marketing companies reach their first six figures in revenue will quickly refer to a business coach specializing in helping high-tech startups scale because these are two very different problems with very different outcomes requiring very different areas of expertise.

Why is it challenging to develop a niche? Many businesses are afraid to work in a niche. They have many offers for people with all kinds of problems, and they think they won't sell as much if they don't help everyone with everything. The nonprofits and for-profit companies I serve have a passion for those they help and don't want to leave anyone behind. Yet when we specialize, the opposite often happens. When we proclaim to the world the specific people we help in precise ways, we can increase our prices and become a lighthouse rather than a tugboat in our market because niching increases our credibility in the marketplace. When you take a lighthouse approach, your company will attract ideal clients or program participants, and you won't feel like you need to push your offer on anyone with a pulse. Yes, you risk leaving some customers behind, but there are enough businesses in the world for someone else to serve those customers in better ways than you could as a generalist.

> Credible offers make it easy for people to say, "I KNOW THE EXACT PERSON FOR YOU!"
>
> — Laura Meyer

When you take a lighthouse approach, potential customers actively seek you out because your brand and messaging act as beacons to attract people with a specific problem. When buyers seek solutions, they value that specificity and will invest a premium. In niching, we have to be okay with letting someone not be a customer. It takes a certain level of confidence to say, "This is what I do," and be willing to refer out a lead if it's not a perfect fit.

Struggling to niche down or communicate the unique transformation you provide to your clients? Here's an exercise I often recommend to my consulting clients. Challenge yourself to niche down with what I call the "Three P's."

The first P is the *problem*: What specific, tangible problem do you solve? You'll know it's specific enough when you can outline measurable before and after metrics in your clients' finances, health, wellness, or relationships. Because I do much work in the personal development space, I understand that intangible offers related to mental health and relationships are tricky. Still, they allow us to be creative and develop a measurement system unique to your business.

The second P is the *person*. In other words, what describes the person you're looking for in specific terms? For example, it's one thing to say you're looking for executives, but it's altogether different from targeting C-suite executives looking for their next promotion. It's one thing to say your market is moms, but far better to say your market is postpartum moms struggling to retain energy after childbirth. You can look for entrepreneurs, but it's much clearer to look for specific entrepreneurs at a precise stage in business.

When it comes to establishing credibility, take a LIGHTHOUSE approach to marketing ♡

— Laura Meyer

The third P is *process*. In my consulting company, I developed a signature methodology called Next Level L.E.A.P. (**L**imit focus; **E**stablish a plan; create **A**ssets; review **P**rogress) that I use to serve clients and certify consultants. Developing a process like Next Level L.E.A.P. takes time and experience. Still, once you have your intellectual property, you have an area of differentiation that no one else can touch.

If you can niche for a specific problem, person, or process, you're well on your way to developing marketplace credibility. Bonus points if you can nail down all three!

BUILDING TRUST BY COMMUNICATING YOUR VALUES

So many of us choose the business we're in because something inside us believes that we can make a difference, do things in a way that will impact others positively, and do things better. The nonprofits I serve are unique because when they speak, their passion for what they stand for and why it's essential is magnetic and compelling. Suppose you don't feel this effect when you talk about your company. In that case, you may also want to begin developing a unique perspective, something that's particularly important in speaking partnerships like joint ventures and podcast exchanges because your unique perspective is what makes your point of view interesting, captivating, and memorable to your ideal client.

My client Tresa Todd has had phenomenal success in the traditionally male-dominated real estate investment education industry with her Women's Real Estate Investment Network program. She credits this success to leading with values. Tresa speaks boldly about ethics and doing the right thing in every workshop and masterclass she teaches. During her sales presentations, Tresa is unapologetic about whom she wants to join her and whom she does not want to join her. She says, "There are plenty of other places to learn real estate— this is the kind of woman I am looking for. I only want positive, ambitious, goal-oriented women committed to mentally, emotionally, spiritually, financially, and physically growing, who are committed to inspiring, encouraging, and empowering."[4] She only wants to work with women who want to make a positive impact. She speaks boldly about her faith in God.

Initially, it was hard for her to be that bold because she wasn't sure how others would respond to such a strong message. But when she realized that people were hungry for that level of leadership in their lives, she spoke out about her faith, inviting into her program women with whom she could build mutual trust because their values were aligned. Every week she receives emails from clients who say that she's changed their lives not only in real estate but also their personal lives, helping them learn to pray and understand scripture. For Tresa, the most exciting thing about her business is having this kind of impact on her clients. Some people join her workshops and promptly opt out, saying that they didn't come to hear about God. That's fine with Tresa; her team happily refunds them. Leading with faith and values is such a core aspect of Tresa's business that it flows out of her in every interaction.

Without communicating our beliefs, it's easy to blend in and be lost in the crowd because we haven't laid out a stance on our businesses' way and why. When you lead with your beliefs and values, it's easier to see others as potential collaborators than competitors. For example, there are many health coaching companies. Still, yours is the only one with your unique viewpoint, values, and beliefs. This perspective will help you better understand how to leverage the community around you to advance your business. The more unpopular your opinions are with the wrong crowd of potential customers and partners, the more popular they will be with the right ones.

We often hesitate to share our viewpoint because we feel pressured to anticipate trends—the approaches we see people taking, how we see offers being presented, and how marketing is carried out. You might believe that if you don't do and say the same things, you'll be left behind—you won't be considered for available opportunities. We often don't realize the effect of this subtle peer pressure and how much it hurts our overall marketplace message.

Perhaps you hold back on sharing your convictions because you're worried about what others might think. You might think that if you share your experience, they won't follow you anymore, or they might think you're weird. But alternative viewpoints are becoming the norm, not the exception. Look at Gwyneth Paltrow as an example. She has historically branded herself as a mainstream celebrity, produced a Netflix series on psychedelics, and marketed candles that smell like part of the female anatomy (which, for the record, I do not own). Taking her as an example, you can see that there is certainly plenty of room for you to share your core values without feeling like a total oddball!

We develop credibility in the marketplace by sharing our values and personal journey because we naturally seek out people who share our values or who have experienced similar challenges. They are our best partners, customers, and collaborators. Most businesses don't lead with values and beliefs in their communications or neutralize their origin story (more on this later in chapter 5) because they're afraid of making waves or attracting too much attention. You need to know what you believe if you're going to build a brand of significance. If you don't share what it is that makes your brand unique—your convictions, your beliefs, either personally or professionally—it will be harder for people to find something to connect with you on a deeper level. Some people start by sharing their personal beliefs, which become part of their personal brand; others share strictly within the realm of their business.

Take a moment to answer the following questions about the core beliefs that were behind your decision to dedicate your professional life to your particular business:

- What are the core values that inspired you to start your business?
- What do you believe about what is possible for you and those you serve?
- What is your driving motivator?
- What does your audience not know about your journey?
- What part of your story would make people feel less alone or relieved if they heard about it?

Now, ask yourself the following:

- Are you telling these stories in the market?
- Are you sharing your beliefs with your audience?
- Are your beliefs deeply ingrained in your brand to the point that when someone is looking at two purchasing options, they're selecting you because they know your story, your motivations for running your business, and the core convictions reflected in how you work with clients?

> **FREE RESOURCE**
>
> Writer's block? We've got you! Visit createyourwinwin.com and get our 37 templates that help to build your authority online with a core message.

This is what will attract clients to you. By contrast, if you're trying to do what everyone else is doing or hesitating to share your core beliefs, you can't help the people you're meant to serve. The point isn't to state your core values in an official poster and share an infographic about them online. The point is to share things that will make your ideal clients feel relieved or less alone because they realize they're not the only ones with that life experience.

If you're having a difficult time with this concept, I want to challenge your thinking by asking you this: over the long term, are you going to build a brand of significance? If your message is generic, it isn't transformative. It's tough to build an authority-based brand without differentiating factors; these factors most often come from attributes related to your journey. Your beliefs, the fundamental aspects of your business, either attract or repel potential clients, collaborators, and partners. There are certain people we gravitate to, not because of their titles or professional backgrounds—although that helps to lead the conversation—but because of what we stand for and against. Our shared values and experience are what create meaningful connections.

As a final word on this topic, if you're going through something challenging, I believe you should share your scars and not your wounds. In other words, wait until the situation has passed and use it as an opportunity to help others once you're on the other side of the experience. If you can't communicate from a place of neutrality, you're not ready to share. Once you've moved through a challenge and can see it as a harrowing experience yet a big blessing, you're prepared to share your journey in a way that can inspire and help others.

CREATING CREDIBLE CONNECTIONS

One of the most significant benefits of relationship marketing is that you can yield many benefits without compromising your values or feeling pressure to participate in trends that don't align with your beliefs. When you lead with your values, you can build proper relationships and a brand that stands out because everyone knows where you stand. Lead with your values, communicate them—don't be afraid to lay it all out there. This will help you identify win-win connections from a values standpoint while leading potential collaborators to you. Many businesses rely on more hands-off marketing channels and aren't designed for the level of intimacy that sets the stage for meaningful conversations and attracts the best collaborators. So if this kind of thinking is new to you, consider these essential questions:

- What transformation does your offer provide?
- Where are you bringing people from, and where are you taking them to?
- How are you going to bring them there with what you're sharing?
- What core principles essential to you will attract or repel certain types of people based on whether or not they share those beliefs?
- What do you want to be known for, above and beyond being a copywriting company, a design agency, a best-selling author, a coach, a marketer, and so on?
- What do you want people to think of when they first hear your name?
- What are the feelings you want to evoke in people?
- How can you be more intentional about conveying your convictions?

Intentionally and thoughtfully being known is crucial to generating referrals and finding the right partnerships to grow your business strategically.

Developing credibility through magnetic messaging is the first step in creating win-win partnerships because credibility created by sharing authentically creates goodwill in the marketplace. As you build your credibility, you'll create a reputation as someone who

Credible offers make it easy for people to say, "I KNOW THE EXACT PERSON FOR YOU!"

—Laura Meyer

isn't just hunting for the next sale but as someone who has value to contribute to the industry. Over time, you'll no longer be worried about what your activity today will give you tomorrow. Instead of being driven by fear, you'll be part of flipping the script and creating a robust win-win ecosystem that catapults its members forward like no other form of marketing can.

> **FREE RESOURCE**
>
> Stuck with a niching problem? Visit createyourwinwin.com and get my three messaging templates that you can try out as you niche down your marketing message.

CHAPTER SUMMARY

We realize that we need to build win-win relationships, but where do we start? First, we must make new connections to be helpful and create value for the other party. We develop these relationships by building trust. To build trust, we must communicate clearly about the specific problems and people we serve, and share our beliefs and values, personally and professionally. This sets us up for success in relationship marketing so that when we implement a win-win, its effectiveness is maximized.

CHAPTER 3

INITIATING THE WIN-WIN

I first met Jennifer Allwood, a popular faith-based influencer and author with a massive online following, at a conference for advanced entrepreneurs called Iconic. At the time, I knew who Jennifer was because of her prominent online presence, but it's safe to say she had no clue who I was. As we mingled in our cocktail party best at the exclusive gathering in Scottsdale, I began assisting a new colleague at our table with an investment decision she was making. The colleague was delighted by my offer to help and exclaimed, "I've invested tens of thousands of dollars in coaching to find the answer to a question that you just helped me with within 10 minutes!" Overhearing our conversation, Jennifer started asking me a bit more about myself, and we began discussing her growth goals. Out of my desire to create value for her, our discovery that we had friends in common, and our realization that we shared the same Christian faith, a foundation of trust was established.

The following day, we agreed to have coffee, not because I wanted her as a client or to take advantage of her follower count but because I was genuinely curious about her business and how I might be able to provide value. After having coffee together, Jennifer became a client for two years, a source of endless referrals to my business, and she remains a dear friend and collaborator to this day.

This is how win-win partnerships take place, not by shaking Jennifer's hand and forcing my business card into her pocketbook or asking her to have coffee with me. (An aside—Jennifer has 100k Instagram followers that would love to have coffee with her.) She observed me creating value for my colleague and saw that I sought to create value for her; the credibility that my actions established continued to develop as we deepened our connection around the common ground of faith and business.

When initiating a win-win relationship, we begin by establishing trust and building credibility, as mentioned previously. When I interact with someone new, I like to play a game in my head that I call, "How quickly can I be helpful to you?" I immediately think about how I can create value for the person I'm interacting with instead of prioritizing how they can benefit me or approaching the exchange with any type of agenda. I simply start by being generous.

My number one goal when I meet someone is to listen actively to find out what they're struggling with or where their unmet needs are. The struggle may be in their business or their personal life. In your interactions with others, if you listen carefully, you will find areas where you can create value. Most people make a mistake because they're looking for an opportunity to market themselves instead of seeking to create value.

Value creation sets the foundation for a win-win.

> **PRO TIP**
>
> Stuck on how to get conversations going when you meet a potential win-win partner? You're not alone. I hear this so often that I created a conversation starter toolkit available at createyourwinwin.com.

As your reputation grows, people will start seeking you out because they know you're a strong connector and generous with whom you know. Consider these two contrasting recommendations for Nancy, who works in publishing:

"I was speaking with Nancy, and she gave me some excellent advice about marketing my book that I hadn't considered. You might want to check with her on the book you're writing or hire her as a speaker for the conference you're working on."

"You should try Nancy. She's in my referral network."

The first is, obviously, a more powerful recommendation, and it came out of Nancy creating value for her colleague.

When developing a new relationship, I prioritize establishing credibility by building trust and communicating specificity in my messaging. I'm never worried about comparing numbers of fans, followers, and likes; instead, I listen intently and think about the value that can be created.

GIVERS, TAKERS, AND MATCHERS

I hope I've sold you on the idea that relationships in your business must be a primary focus if you want sustainable, long-term growth. Now, let's consider how to begin building new connections in a way that builds relationships rather than leave us feeling like we need to shower. The source of that slimy feeling is often an imbalance of expectations. Many business owners struggle because they're either too much of a giver, that is, they're overly generous but secretly resentful toward those who take from them without reciprocating, or they're present only to take from you, that is wanting to know how fast they can get a client out of you, and if it's not instant, they move on.

In his 2013 best-selling book *Give and Take*, renowned organizational psychologist Adam Grant describes people as either takers, givers, or matchers in terms of how they typically approach social interactions.[1,2] Takers usually strive to get as much as possible from others and are driven by self-serving motives. They ask, "What can you do for me?" Givers, however, typically contribute to others without expecting anything in return. They ask, "What can I do for you?" They're generous, often to a fault.

Matchers sit in the middle. They have a quid pro quo mindset, willing to help but expect something in return. So, which one should we be?

Interestingly, Grant found that although givers occupy the bottom of the success ladder, they're also the ones on top. The highest echelons of success belong to givers, those who are ready to help others with no strings attached. Givers most often elevate their companies and effect positive societal change. And as Grant put it, when givers succeed, people celebrate *with* them instead of gunning for them. They inspire others also to give, creating a culture of giving.

For those extra generous, the question becomes, "How do I become a successful giver? How do I avoid burnout and being taken advantage of?" The answer is to be a giver with boundaries—someone who knows when and how to give and to whom.

Counterintuitively, the problem that many of us have is that we need to be better at asking and receiving. Win-wins become blocked for us because, deep down, we are terrible at receiving. We see a self-fulfilling prophecy in our relationships; we think, "Oh, all the people around me are just takers." In actuality, we are simply bad at receiving. We enter communities expecting people to take from us, attracting the takers. We're unclear about what we want, and yet, what we often want is a win-win.

With the right mindset, we are naturally attracted to givers. Givers are the power connectors with whom we all want to get to know better and form reciprocal relationships. They have extraordinary professional contacts because they love seeing others win. They are always trying to recall whom they know would be a fantastic introduction for their most recent connection. Because of that generosity, the desire to reciprocate grows, and win-win relationships form. For this reason, when thinking about a business fueled by relationships, I recommend you surround yourself with three different types of connections.

The first type of connection is one in which you're purely generous; it's with those who are a couple of steps behind you and are part of your audience. You inspire them. You can be of service to them. You can help them. I'm not saying that you have to get on a phone call with everyone that needs your help (please don't!). Still, if you're creating regular content like teaching materials and posts, these connections validate your offering by growing your fanbase and highlighting your generosity. Because they're the people you're working to help, they can give you clues about how you can serve in a better way and help your ideal clients solve their biggest problems. They become your best clients and advocates, the biggest supporters of what you create, sharing it with their peers. They're members of your audience—podcast listeners, book readers—not necessarily purchasers of your offer but love what you do and are happy to share it with anyone who will listen.

Being a giver through content creation and even writing books like this allows you to be generous to those a few steps behind you while simultaneously building up goodwill in your industry. It's your way of contributing to the greater good and providing inspiration through your story. You can use feedback from your audience as you write books and create podcasts and blog posts for people who need your help.

When you're of service to someone and give them something in advance, you bank years of loyalty in return. Don't be surprised if, someday, a person who was a couple of steps behind you is at your level or has catapulted forward. Then you have a great relationship you wouldn't have had otherwise.

This exact situation unfolded between Tanya Dalton and me. You might be familiar with her; she has won multiple awards and had one of the top books in business last year, *The Joy of Missing Out*. She has had success after success. But I met Tanya before all her accomplishments when she came to me with a request. Tanya was starting a jewelry business at the time, and I happened to have a large multi-location retail operation. Before long, I became her best customer because I believed in her. I saw something unique in her and knew she could do tremendous things. I saw her incredible raw talent, brilliance, and tenacity and immediately desired to support her business.

A couple of years later, I closed my retail business (through which I had been her best customer). Tanya had also moved on, developing an online e-commerce company that catapulted her into superstar status. Her best-selling book created a tidal wave of publicity and recognition. Now I had a fantastic relationship with someone who was way ahead of me, right when I was moving away from retail and transitioning into online entrepreneurship. She helped me become visible in a new industry; she was the first guest on my podcast, and she introduced me to several of her powerful CEO friends. This story illustrates a fundamental principle of building relationships that so many miss. When it comes to relationships, you're playing the long game, and you never know when a great connection will come back to you.

When it comes to relationships, you're playing the long game, AND YOU NEVER KNOW *when generosity will come back to you.*

— Laura Meyer

The second type of people you want to surround yourself with are those who are exactly where you are. These people have a similar following and similar audience size. They'll be your collaborators or matchers. Because they have a similar audience size, they'll be excited about collaborating with you, realizing that your work will be mutually beneficial and strategic.

This takes having a certain level of confidence in what we are capable of and what our organizations can bring into a relationship. Although this book is not about building confidence (nor am I a confidence expert), I can share my experience with you. You'll often be surprised by how much you know, by how much you can contribute to a conversation, even at high-level events, on popular podcasts, or in communities filled with advanced experts. As a thoughtful, intelligent, sensitive human uniquely created by God, your gifts, abilities, and most importantly, your experiences can make a difference for someone in ways that you rarely recognize or understand and in ways that you tend to underestimate until you see it happen. That's why it's so important to be courageous in making new connections. With your newfound courage, confidence will come over time.

The popular idea that we can only collaborate with people who are farther along than us because they'll bring us exposure is mistaken because it is much more common for our contemporaries to be our co-creators. Your contemporaries are people you'll be speaking at summits with; you'll be on each other's podcasts and bring out new talents and ideas in one another. Being part of a community with these peers is extremely valuable when you need someone who understands where you are in your business and can help you brainstorm ideas, move through roadblocks, and gain insight from someone living your current reality. Contemporary relationships are elevated over time because you rise together by collaborating, sharing, brainstorming, and connecting. Being able to look back at someone who was there with you and say, "Remember when…" and "Look at us now" is beautiful.

Finally, surround yourself with leaders you look up to and aspire to be like, people who you look at and think, "Wow, that's fantastic. They've created an incredible outcome that I'm so excited by." Based on the number of nasty social media comments I've seen on my own and my client's social media platforms, I know that many individuals struggle with a scarcity mindset. They see business as a zero-sum game and have difficulty being excited for and inspired by those who have achieved the level of success or recognition they desire. Yet, when we choose to be thrilled for those we look up to, knowing that business is not a zero-sum game but an incredible opportunity for blessing and abundance, we have a greater chance of being in a relationship with them.

When you connect with those organizations and leaders ahead of you, you will not immediately collaborate with them simply because you aren't at their experience level. For example, it's not probable that I'll be able to message Oprah Winfrey and invite her to a podcast exchange (but Oprah, if you're reading this, *call me!*) These are not relationships based on reciprocity because you may not yet be in a position to have much to offer. Instead, you might send a message to this kind of connection and say, "I want to let you know that you inspire me. I love your content. I appreciate you for being part of this world and showing me an example of what's possible."

These simple messages go a long way. In the rare instances, I receive messages like this, I don't forget them. They make me think, "Wow, what a gracious, generous person. What an incredible human to realize that I'm somewhere they want to be, but they aren't jealous or threatened; they are inspired. I'll keep my eye on this person because they're going somewhere." It takes a notable amount of humility and confidence to send that kind of message.

In exchanges with connections, it's essential to understand the difference between the three types of connections and be clear on what is possible, what you're looking to achieve, and how you can contribute to them while leading with your values and your mission in life. Sometimes we discover that our goals don't match those of a connection because we've been unclear about what we want to accomplish in business or have unrealistic expectations. An actual win-win business relationship is with someone whose goals match or overlap ours.

Remember, the time to start contacting these three different types of connections is *not* when you need your next client. This inadvertently leads to an extraction mindset (see chapter 1), which is the number one credibility killer in relationship marketing. You cannot meet people today and expect them to hire, refer, or partner with you immediately. Begin building relationships by establishing credibility in the marketplace; don't wait until you need relationship marketing to work or you have an extensive program where you're looking for affiliate partners. Now is the time to start making connections so that when you have a gap in your client roster or your Facebook ad account gets shut down, you'll have already developed credibility with a group of people who know the perfect next client for you.

GROWING RELATIONSHIP CAPITAL

As we begin to establish credibility and learn how to identify which of our new connections are peers, we can move into the second phase of the win-win formula, which is all about increasing visibility for your business among your peers, potential partners, and best-fit clients.

This move into the visibility stage will be most effective, lucrative, and impactful. For me, you will conduct the most enjoyable marketing effort in your organization. Once you've gone through a credibility audit in your organization using the previous chapter as a guide, you are ready to start establishing key partners and partner activities that will grow your company through visibility.

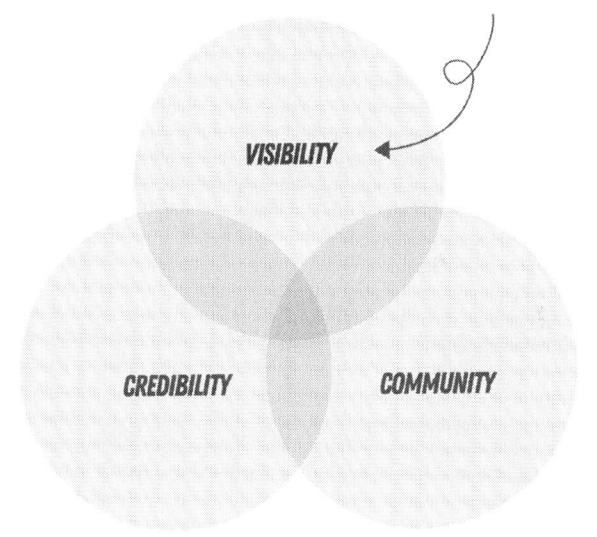

Win-Win FORMULA

Venn diagram showing three overlapping circles labeled VISIBILITY, CREDIBILITY, and COMMUNITY

When finding companies or organizations to partner with in creating win-win partnerships, most of the people you interact with will be peers, which presents endless matching opportunities. When interacting with peer companies, consider how you can exchange platforms by being on each other's podcasts. We will cover this in-depth in chapters 4 and 5. As trust is built, you will often become referral partners or co-creators. You may even work on a project together to create a better outcome for a client, which neither one of you could provide on your own. The goal with anyone that you match up with is a value exchange.

The second category of interaction that increases visibility is with people who look up to you. It's imperative that you don't lose sight of them as you grow your company. I've been an entrepreneur for a long time. There have been moments when I was someone well-known in an industry, speaking on stage to thousands of people, and other moments when I was not prominent. As your visibility increases and your reputation grows, more and more people will contact you because they're inspired by you or want your advice and help. The mistake many companies make is to treat such connections as matchers. Having people reach out is a good sign that you're growing a fantastic reputation and doing the right things to increase your visibility.

You need to treat these exchanges a little bit differently. You might send kind words or quick advice. Maybe they have a question you can feature in your podcast, Instagram stories, or blog. They may have a problem you haven't even thought about that might inspire you on a tough day when your marketing department needs to send an email to the subscriber list, or your content writer's material is falling flat, and you need to give them fresh ideas. You might send free teaching materials, a webinar, video, or an information session to create goodwill without giving up your personal boundaries. The mistake many people make is thinking that people in this category are just takers looking to get something from you, which isn't true.

Knowing how to navigate these two types of relationships—those your company matches and those you give to—is very important. To do so, you need to understand the difference between your audience and customer profiles. Both are important to your company's success, but they play two different roles in the growth of your business. Those who fit your audience profile are those you give to; they're critical to growing visibility for your business. These people read your books, listen to and review your podcasts, and buy your merchandise. They may not be your ideal client, but they know someone who is, and your goal in every one of these interactions is to inspire loyalty.

Your ideal customer is aware of their problem and actively seeking a solution. They may be weighing different options to solve their problem and may or may not know that your specific solution exists. They're the financial fuel for your company and will enter into your marketing or sales processes to make a decision. From that point, it's your job to ensure that they make the right decision, regardless of whether it benefits your company in the short term.

The third category of interaction is with people we aspire to work with; with these connections, seek to increase your visibility with them. Think about the different ways you can create value for them. Listen; observe what they're experiencing; consider how you can get their attention. High-level authors, thought leaders, and influencers receive message after message, day after day. Most of them never leave the junk folder. So how do you get noticed?

Here are some ways to get started:

- Observe their businesses first, and then ask for an introduction from someone affiliated with them, a trusted source, or someone who either works for them or is in their networking circles. Find an event they'll be speaking at or participating in and ask in advance for an introduction. Help in an area where they can use service—*no strings attached.*
- Don't ask too soon or outside of what would be considered reasonable. Remember that for busy potential partners, the most valuable asset they have is not their money but

their time. Never ask for their time without them clearly understanding how it would benefit them.
- Be grateful and positive. Understand that how you handle yourself in the marketplace communicates to the influencer whether or not you're a risk. They might be inclined to believe that most new connections will try to use them to get ahead; show them that you are different. You're indeed working on getting to know them so that you can borrow their influence, but you also want the best for them. Your number one goal is to create a win-win situation, not to take advantage. Many of my contacts in this category have gone from being dream connections to paying customers using this strategy.

My friend Aryeh Sheinbein is a master relationship builder and finance genius who brokers multimillion dollar Wall Street deals while holding a fascinatingly diverse portfolio of personal investments. Outside of his impressive, traditional job, he invests in Amazon shops, offers a variety of advisory services to entrepreneurs, and coordinates large-scale commercial property investments.

A great observer of industry trends with extensive expertise in growing Amazon shops,

Aryeh noticed that John, a well-known and very popular business influencer, was selling his journals on Amazon. John is known for his financial transparency and publishes his quarterly results online. Curious about his approach to business, Aryeh started commenting and engaging with his online content. After a while, Aryeh reached out to John on Instagram through a direct message. Although John receives hundreds, if not thousands, of pitches and direct messages daily, Aryeh's was different. First, Aryeh's name was already recognizable because of his comments and support. Second, Aryeh made John a video taking note of John's Amazon shop numbers and explaining how John could increase his earnings. John was intrigued, shared his email address, and within 24 hours, Aryeh's advice had increased what he was receiving from Amazon. Trust was immediately established between the two of them. John became a long-term colleague of Aryeh's, a connection that amplified Aryeh's credibility in the business world.

Here you can see that knowing the difference between the three categories of interaction is critically important to increasing visibility. How Aryeh approached John is very different than how we developed our relationship, which grew from a friendly and informal peer-to-peer connection. When finding potential partners for your next win-win, think about how you can be intentional based on which category your potential partner fits into.

Every company I consult with—nonprofit or for-profit, big or small—has its dream list of customers or collaborators. No matter what type of person you're dealing with, be confident that you can create value for them. Here are some tips on how to seek out value creation for potential collaborators:

- Take notice of which category of connection you're dealing with in any given situation and be aware of your role. Sometimes people misstep or make gaffes because they misread their role and go in too soon, without enough relationship capital built.
- Be thoughtful about audiences. Sometimes people dismiss audience members, discounting their value and importance and not realizing their critical role. Notice what's possible in each interaction and challenge yourself to think creatively about each type.

From there, your reputation as a great person or company to be connected to will multiply.

HOW COLLABORATIONS INCREASE VISIBILITY

As you grow trust and credibility in the marketplace, you'll begin growing the three types of connections. Most of the win-win collaborations you'll develop will be with your peers.

When we think about whom to collaborate with without a focus, we risk only collaborating with companies or leaders we simply find exciting or personally like. Such connections make great colleagues and friends to go to lunch with and can be great for peer-to-peer feedback. Still, they're often not ideal in terms of developing collaborations that grow our visibility in the eyes of our target audience.

When brainstorming about who would be a great collaborator or lead generation partner for developing a win-win relationship, consider other companies who solve problems for your ideal client. For this approach to work, it's essential to have a niche and a unique viewpoint, as mentioned previously, so if you haven't done that work yet, now is the time to dig in! When you niche, you'll realize that where your collaborator's clients' problems begin or end is where your services pick up. For example, if someone needs a bookkeeper, whom better to ask for a recommendation than a CPA? For a CPA to provide expert tax advice, they need the financials to be in good order, which requires a bookkeeper. Another example is a health or wellness coach who helps pregnant women; they may end up partnering with a health or wellness company that assists postpartum women or provides newborn care. Without fail, every company I help to grow through relationship marketing vastly underestimates whom they are already connected to and how that connection could turn into a win-win.

EXERCISE

Not sure who would be a great collaborator for you? Ponder these questions:

- What happens before clients need your services?
- What do they need to believe?
- What do they need to be working toward?
- What problems do they have?
- What are they aspiring to?

Next, think about clients after they graduate from your services.

- Where do they go next?
- What do they need assistance with after you're finished working with them?

Still stuck on finding partners? Make a list of...

- Those you've worked with in previous roles
- People you've met at past events or conferences
- Your LinkedIn or social media connections
- Expired clients or program alumni
- Peers in CEO groups or programs you've attended
- Client leads never followed up with

If you do this exercise right, I guarantee you're underestimating the number of companies and organizations to which you are already connected. These connections are seeking their own win-win partnerships and would be thrilled to hear from you.

FINDING WIN-WIN PARTNERS

Win-win partnerships can take many forms. They can be developed with audience partners; you can feature on one another's platforms to generate new leads. They can be created with partners who offer direct referrals to your business simply because they trust you and want the best for the client. They can also be developed with joint-venture partners or affiliates. In this scenario, partners take a percentage of sales in exchange for a referral. Creating win-win partnerships begins with marketplace credibility—built up by utilizing the strategies provided in the previous chapters—reinforced by visibility built up through collaborations. The work of niching and increasing the effectiveness of your offer will strengthen your reputation as you begin to collaborate. Without niching and increasing the effectiveness of your offer, potential collaborators may start working with you, only to conclude that there isn't as much substance to your offer as they thought.

You've done the hard work of establishing credibility. Now, who makes a great collaboration partner? Ideal collaborators are found in businesses that serve the same audience as you but solve different problems. For example, in my program, Fractional Freedom, I train my consulting students how to be fractional chief marketing officers or growth consultants so that clients they serve can benefit from high-level marketing strategy support without making a C-suite executive hire. That offer is a massive win-win in itself! Other fractional C-suite providers, for example, fractional chief operating officers, fractional chief financial officers, and fractional chief human resource officers, are great collaborators for a fractional chief marketing officer because client companies are not only at a similar stage of business development, but they've also bought into the business model of using fractional C-suite hires.

A relationship and marriage support program might work well with a travel agency. Both serve the same audience—couples prioritizing their relationships—but they solve different problems for these couples. Couples go to a relationship therapist for help with their marriages; a travel agent helps create romantic vacations that give them the time and space to work on their relationships.

A copywriting company would be well served by partnering with a graphic design firm because to communicate effectively on sales pages, copy needs good graphic design. Often, buyers run comprehensive marketing campaigns or direct response marketing efforts in which they simultaneously hire a copywriter and a graphic designer. These two occupations serve the same audience but help with different problems.

There can also be good collaboration between people who are different but complement one another, for example, people with different personalities, skill sets, or perspectives. It's essential to be creative and operate from a mindset of thinking about what's possible. I know two branding specialists with diverse backgrounds who approach their work from very different perspectives. Martha Cristina Garza, one of my consulting students in Fractional Freedom, comes from a luxury product, hospitality, and retail marketing background. She brings a particular flair to her work with product providers. Also, she has her own jewelry line, which adds further credibility to her product-based experience, as she tends to be exclusively dedicated to the luxury product space. The other specialist, Zaneera Azlan, is a brand storytelling expert and marketing strategist with broad cross-industry experience in the corporate and nonprofit sectors. She has held brand and marketing roles globally with United Nations, FMCG companies, and in the emerging tech industry. Azlan currently offers her consulting services to professional services firms and entrepreneurs who want compelling brand storytelling and cross-platform marketing strategies for business areas that are a bit more complicated in nature.

Many times, these two women partner up or refer clients to each other, and I'm always in awe of how they're able to see community over competition because that's something that many experts struggle to fully embrace. In theory, both women could help the same client and do a fantastic job. By leaning into their unique personalities, skill sets, and perspectives, they're able to attract perfect clients and repel unsuitable ones. This ultimately builds the reach of their businesses and creates deeper satisfaction in their work. Because of this mindset, they can refer best-fit clients to one another.

Another characteristic of great collaborators is that they're people whose values align with yours. For example, a faith-based health coaching company will have a great values connection with a faith-based business coaching company. That's not to say that everyone in the health coach's audience will be an excellent fit for business coaching and vice versa. Still, their shared faith values will be interesting, compelling, and valuable to both audiences. Suppose you have the same beliefs, philosophies, and commitment to a particular set of values as someone else. In that case, chances are you can contribute to each other's audiences in a relevant way. Although not everyone in your collaborator's audience will be an ideal client, they're likely to know someone who is.

Many companies struggle to consider where to find potential collaborators while vastly underestimating the number of people to whom they are connected. Here are some areas to consider looking at if you're struggling for ideas.

Past or current clients

Many of your historical or current clients make fantastic collaboration or referral partners, even if they knew you in a different industry or role. They could have been clients when you were working for another company and now have their own companies or platforms or are connected to organizations that would now make fantastic partners for you. As you saw from my example at the beginning of chapter 1, my peers in one stage of my entrepreneurial journey became clients in the next phase. This exercise would also work for former employees or bosses with whom you still have a cordial relationship.

Social media contacts

I've often heard those new to relationship marketing state that they aren't networked well with ideal customers or don't know many people. At that moment, I challenge them to export their LinkedIn connections into a spreadsheet or look at their Facebook contacts individually. They are often shocked to realize that they have an excellent set of contacts they have forgotten about or didn't realize are now in a leadership role at a new company that would be ideal for outreach. We often feel pressure to meet new people and try to get connected while underestimating the excellent set of contacts we already have.

Live events

I find live events the best way to meet new people and contacts. When I'm at a live event, I try to ensure that I go in knowing a few people, even if I introduce myself to them virtually first and schedule a few coffee chats or lunches in advance to get the momentum going. Events where the room is prequalified, such as being a C-suite executive to attend or having a business with a minimum revenue, tend to make for the best connection opportunities. Many live events have free social media groups or virtual chat previews before the event, where you can get introductions started before arrival. I recently attended an event where I posted that I was looking for people to play tennis with at the conference and met some fantastic connections without even meaning to do so. The gym is also a great place to network in the morning for those who enjoy fitness activities.

After a live event, take the time to connect with each person on your preferred platform, like LinkedIn, so that you can continue to build a relationship and stay in touch after the event has ended.

Networking organizations

Networking organizations vary significantly in terms of how well they are run, the degree to which people who attend are vetted, and the participation requirements. When entering a networking organization, pay attention to the culture and values of the community and see if you can try out a few meetings to get a sense of who is in the room. While I have been part of networking organizations and even led one for a while, they can be tricky regarding what type of personal dynamics are taking place. I recommend investing our time in organizations focused on collaboration and connection versus those that force referrals before trust is built.

There are many other ways to meet potential collaborators, such as joining nonprofit boards, participating in charity work, taking up a social sport like golf, pickleball, paddle, or tennis if you're looking for local connections, social media outreach to like-minded companies, or being part of masterminds and coaching programs. Many leaders think they have much work to do when finding the right connections to collaborate. Still, it's usually more a matter of taking the time to consider who they already know and are connected to.

THE SECRET TO GROWING YOUR VISIBILITY

Many businesses are fantastic at making their customers happy, but those same companies tend to be the best-kept secret around. Why? Because they struggle to gain visibility or think that visibility is only made possible through significant public relations investments. There is a time and place for public relations, but it's possible to utilize uncomplicated tools and resources to increase your visibility without much investment. As your credibility and visibility grow, a multiplier effect kicks in, and you'll see an increase in qualified leads flowing into your company.

Here's an illustration for those who like to see how things work from a mathematical perspective. Consider the number of people needing to see your offer in a paid advertisement to convert ten sales. A reasonable click-through rate on a paid ad for a for-profit company is around 1 percent–3 percent, so you need to purchase placements that can generate hundreds of thousands of views simply to get 100 leads into your sales process. Depending on the effectiveness of your sales process, you might get 20–30 people to see your offer, and an even smaller fraction will convert into a sale. Consumers are smart. They are aware when they're being targeted by advertisements, and sophisticated buyers tend to approach paid advertisements with a high level of skepticism, even if they address an unmet need.

By contrast, if your ideal customers are listening to a particular podcast or reading a confident thought leader's content on LinkedIn, you can reach them using platforms they already trust as a delivery vehicle. When you do so, your credibility grows. If one of those ideal clients hears you on another podcast, you're validated again. Increased visibility will make your entire sales process more effective, even if your audience numbers are lower. In addition, relationship marketing is much more cost-effective than paid advertising. When you combine relationship marketing with paid advertising, your advertisements will perform more effectively because when the target audience sees your ads, it won't be the first time they've heard of you.

MAXIMIZING VISIBILITY THROUGH COLLABORATIONS

There's a little-known secret about how visibility works to grow businesses—a powerful psychological phenomenon called the mere exposure effect.[3] The principle of the mere exposure effect is that people tend to prefer things they're familiar with. Why? Because repeated exposure increases trust. The more someone sees your brand on social media platforms, podcasts, and speaking events, the more they develop a preference for you and your business. The mere exposure effect allows us to succeed in business simply by showing up and increasing our visibility. To illustrate this point, when you hear a song for the first time, you think, "Oh, that's a nice song." But by the tenth time you listen to it, you're tapping your foot and singing along because you've come to like it the more you hear it. Suppose you're a parent to a preschooler. In that case, you may be familiar with the catchy tune of a YouTube song that is more than slightly repelling the first time you hear it, but after the twentieth time through, you're bopping along with your child, and you're both smiling like goofballs (or at least that's what happens in my house!).

Peer-to-peer collaborations like podcast exchanges or features on one another's email lists expedite the mere exposure effect. Of course, they increase your visibility to new audiences. But in addition, if a well-liked and trusted person features you, their audience will extend that trust to you, which is often referred to as "borrowed influence." For example, I recently guested on two clients' podcasts that opened the door for their audiences to learn about me and led to several other podcast appearances. The continued familiarity brought me speaking opportunities within their paid coaching programs and generated several referrals from a well-known influencer. This happens when you create habits that increase your exposure and visibility; these habits payout like compound interest as your credibility builds.

The following chapters will highlight the importance of having a platform—a podcast or email list—that you can bring into collaborative exchanges so that you can start taking advantage of the mere exposure effect in your business. Suppose you are a nonprofit organization or having a platform doesn't make sense for your company. In that case, I will share with you some alternative ways to ensure you have something to offer in developing win-win partnerships. Even if you have a minimal platform or audience, with dedication and consistency you can utilize the power of the mere exposure effect to increase your visibility and credibility in the marketplace by showing up more often by partnering with peer organizations.

CHAPTER SUMMARY

When developing a win-win relationship with a new connection, we start by being a giver, bringing value to the other party. We must approach each interaction with an understanding of our role and the type of connection we're dealing with—a peer, someone we're aspiring to emulate, or someone who's in our audience. Most of our collaborative relationships will be with our peers. When we find ways to share platforms and audiences with collaborators mutually, we establish credibility within the marketplace, building the foundation for qualified lead generation and future business growth.

CHAPTER 4

DEVELOPING THE WIN-WIN

If you follow me on social media, you know that I'm an avid tennis player. One fall, as I was getting back into the game, I joined a local doubles team. Two ladies played one court down from me—Jane and Marge. During our season, Marge celebrated her 80th birthday, and Jane casually mentioned that she wasn't too far behind. Despite being in their golden years, Jane and Marge won all their games.

Every. Single. Match.

Curious, I observed them to find out why. Their opponents, often women in their 30s, 40s, and 50s frantically ran around the court, trying to anticipate what Jane and Marge would do next, applying brute force to every attempt at the ball. But Jane and Marge handled each shot like the queens they were. One of them would simply and accurately place the ball in the holes left wide open by their much younger opponents. I'd often hear groans and squeals as their opponents watched a ball fly over their heads and land six inches in or effortlessly in the perfect spot that not even Rafa Nadal could reach. It was hilarious to watch and proved an important lesson: knowing where to place your focus is the key to winning.

As you have discovered by now, to create win-win collaborations in our companies, we often need to undergo specific shifts in our thinking with a new focus. Many marketing or sales experts advise companies to talk to as many people as possible to find someone to hire them or sell their offers through cold outreach and random direct messages. They mistakenly teach that the person in front of you is the person you should be selling to, and sales is simply a numbers game. The (cold) hard truth is that's rarely the case. Not only does this tend to attract the wrong type of long-term prospect for your business (even if it creates a sale in the short term), but it's also an incorrect assumption that everyone you speak to is a potential customer. So instead of seeking connections with potential clients, I'm going to challenge you to start seeking relationships with potential collaborators.

For example, let's say you attend a convention and casually begin a conversation with the person in line for coffee in front of you. You're a marketing agency owner and discover that the person you speak with has an IT (information technology) consulting company. At first glance, it appears to be a simple meeting to pass the time. But as you begin to ask questions, the owner of the IT consulting company is the go-to firm for a venture capital company who regularly acquires new brands, all of whom are weak in the area of marketing talent. It might be that a small joint white labeled project together to build trust with the V.C. company is possible. Even if you don't make much profit on that initial project, it could be a fantastic collaboration that could open up doors down the road.

When we are making new connections, it's possible the person you're in contact with is a Forbes contributor, has a Facebook group of hundreds of people, thousands of followers on Instagram, or 500 connections on LinkedIn, and you have a shared ideal customer, but it's unlikely they're your perfect client. From a numbers and probability standpoint, it is much more likely that they *know* your ideal customer or have those individuals in their audiences than it is that they *are* your ideal customer. The mistake many people make when developing new connections is to automatically assume they should sell to the person in front of them, which is a repellent and squashes any hope of future interactions. They may also dismiss the connection as a simple exchange of pleasantries instead of considering that that person has the high potential to become a collaborator.

This habit doesn't come easy at first, but once you learn how to think creatively when speaking to a new connection, by asking the right questions while establishing credibility, win-win ideas will begin rolling off your tongue. As you discover that a new relationship has the potential as a fantastic collaboration partner consider the following strategies:

- Think about ways in which you can create value for each other's audiences or customer bases through email, video, or other communication channels
- Examine what they're currently doing, be inquisitive, and consider how you can help or contribute
- Brainstorm ways in which your own audience would benefit from their expertise

For example, suppose you connect with someone who has a podcast. Take the time to listen to the podcast before pitching a collaboration opportunity to them or ask them directly what their listeners like to hear about. Think about what hasn't been covered in their podcast and what their audience might want to hear. If you connect with someone with a popular blog or a LinkedIn Live show, consider what you could share that would be helpful, provide a different perspective, and add your unique expertise. How can you help your collaboration partner increase their visibility and yours? If you're interacting with a potential affiliate partner, what other affiliates have they partnered with, and how does your business create unique value for their audience?

> **🔊 PRO TIP**
>
> Once you realize someone is a good connection for you, it's a good idea first to become part of their audience. Share their posts, join their groups, follow them on social media, or subscribe to their podcast. Be committed to what they're doing and engage with them. Always think about how to add value to their world.

In evaluating potential collaborators, it's also good to consider what stage their business is in. For example, in my Fractional Freedom consulting certification program, I train my consulting students to work exclusively with companies that are between one and 20 million dollars in revenue—not to be exclusionary but to cater to the specific problems that exist in that revenue range. My signature system, Next Level L.E.A.P., is a growth process designed to solve common problems within a particular niche. The training I provide helps my students become in-demand specialists for high-growth clients. Once clients outgrow a growth consultant, they need to find in-house talent to take over the strategy. That makes a recruiter a perfect referral partner for a growth consultant once a client is ready to hire someone to handle what the growth consultant does internally. Partnering with someone whose services end where your services begin (or vice versa) is a great collaboration strategy.

COLLABORATION IDEAS

Here are some examples of collaborative exchanges to get you started brainstorming ways to collaborate.

Social Media

Suppose you've created a partnership with someone whose leading platform is Instagram. You could arrange an exchange as simple as a two- or three-minute video in which you introduce each other to your respective audiences. After you present your collaboration partner (and vice versa), they come on video and say, "Thank you so much for that introduction. This is what I do, whom I help, and how I help them."

> **FREE RESOURCE**
>
> Visit createyourwinwin.com to get our social media collaboration campaign. It will get you started with an easy-to-use template.

After the videos are complete, post them to stories or the feed and interact with the viewers, thanking them for watching the videos. This is a simple and easy win-win strategy on Instagram stories that you and a collaborator can put together in a short time. Alternatively, you might go live with one another's audiences on Facebook. Or share written or video interviews on LinkedIn to give each other's audience a way of seeing something from a new perspective or as a pattern interrupt on a topic they've been wondering about. At the end of each exchange, it's a good practice to provide a piece of gated content or a lead magnet so the audience can go to a particular URL and download content that brings them into your audience and adds them to your email list. This lead generation strategy will produce more qualified, engaged leads because the audience is familiar with and trusts your collaborator. When you collaborate with someone, the trust your partner's audience has in them transfers to you and results in much more engaged new members in your audience than you would gain if they found you cold.

> *Relationship marketing allows you to* **STAND OUT** *as a leader in your industry in a way few other investments can.*
>
> — Laura Meyer

> 🔊 **PRO TIP**
>
> The stronger the audience someone has, the more protective they will be of their audience or email list. Be aware that a potential collaborator may look at your social media platforms to ensure you're legitimate and know your stuff. They may want to get to know you better to ensure that you have similar values and care about the same things they do before joining a collaboration. Be patient and allow credibility to build.

Podcasts

Podcasts are another terrific way to collaborate. Influencer Marketing Hub reports, "According to data shared by Statista, almost 60% of all US consumers older than 12 listen to podcasts. What's more, the number of podcast listeners have steadily increased during the past eight years. While it only increased from 55% to 57% in the past year, it has doubled over the last ten years.... Not only are the number of podcasts and listeners increasing, but also the ad revenues. According to eMarketer, it's anticipated that US marketers will spend more than $1.3 billion on podcast ads in 2021. What's more, it's expected that it will exceed the $2 billion mark in two years, and in 2025 it will be closer to $3 billion."[1]

I love podcast guesting and have made it my preferred method of collaboration. You can make guest appearances on other people's podcasts or create your own podcast to offer exchange guesting opportunities. You can grow a podcast to advertise your programs or generate ad revenue from outside sources. At the end of a podcast, it's standard etiquette to ask an interviewee where listeners can go to find out more about their business, allowing podcast guests to send new, qualified leads to their email lists and elegantly invite listeners into sales conversations.

Margy Feldhuhn, CEO of Interview Connections, a top podcast booking agency, says, "Whether you have a podcast or not, consistently guesting on other shows is an incredible way to become more discoverable, more visible, and foster real relationships and connections. Some of the best relationships I have are with people I met through podcast guesting and people who have interviewed me on their podcasts. By being consistent guests on podcasts, our clients have closed high-ticket coaching and consulting clients, attracted major media features, and landed dream speaking engagements."[2]

Guest Blogging

Guest blogging combined with an email list is a powerful way to exchange value with others, which few people consider. If you love to write and enjoy search-optimizing content, writing a blog article (or transcribing an audio recording to a blog article) that is sent to an email list is a fantastic way to collaborate with others. Blogging is also beneficial when combined with other strategies, such as email nurture, in which a search-optimized blog generates new leads for an email list. Then additional emails are sent to establish trust and credibility with the reader.

Meagan Meier Beltekoğlu, a technology automation and strategic planning consultant, and Alexis Perry, an online content creation expert, regularly partner to promote one another online through blogging and social media posts. As a result, they regularly exchange referrals and share new offerings and updates with one another's audiences. Their religious beliefs prevent them from promoting their businesses using images of themselves, so blog exchanges provide them with a creative and effective way to collaborate while continuing to honor their core beliefs and values.

Video Interviews

Video interviews on LinkedIn, YouTube, or other social media platforms can easily resonate with new audiences and build familiarity with your face and brand. You can create video content and stagger its release; you release it to your respective audiences at different times. This gives each interviewee's audience the chance to consume the content at different times, increasing the chances of more people seeing the interview. Once you interview each other, simply distribute the videos via email, YouTube, LinkedIn, Facebook, or other social media channels. Tag your colleague's account so viewers can learn more about their work.

Small Group Masterminds

Napoleon Hill first wrote about "mastermind alliances" in his 1928 book *Think and Grow Rich*.[3] Hill writes that a mastermind is "A friendly alliance with one or more persons who will encourage one to follow through with both plan and purpose."[3] We as individuals can only draw on our own experience; in a mastermind, we can draw on the expertise of a group of like-minded peers. A mastermind amplifies the strengths of each individual in the group and provides encouragement as we pursue our business endeavors.

Being in the right networking organizations or small groups provides opportunities to create value for others. If you hear that a peer has a problem you've helped others with, you can say, "Here's a piece of content I created that you might find helpful." As a result, they may say, "That's amazing! Can I feature you on my platform so that you can share more about that topic with my audience?" Masterminds and small groups are ideal places to meet new collaborators and affiliates for your business. The premise of a mastermind is to establish relationships with other people and build credibility with one another through problem-solving. This creates more powerful connections than those developed through networking. I invest in a mastermind each year, and I continually assess which one is right for me based on the quality of the conversations and connections it provides relative to my stage of business growth.

Exclusive Trainings

An exclusive, one-time training is a fantastic way to create value for a partner's audience and is specifically beneficial in an affiliate partnership. In an affiliate partnership, you can create a live or prerecorded masterclass or presentation that resides within your partner's paid program or free, gated community. Each time a sale is made, the affiliate partner earns a percentage. Affiliate partnerships work best once you have a solid and proven offer with a track record of testimonials or case studies. It also helps clarify how your request complements your partner's offer.

For example, I have several affiliates for my consulting certification program, Fractional Freedom. One trains and certifies copywriters, and another trains paid traffic ad managers. My best consulting students come from business growth backgrounds and already have working marketing knowledge. Many agency owners eventually outgrow using fully outsourced services and want to shift to working on a big-picture strategy. My consulting incubator is perfect for such students. My students are thrilled because they're learning a skill set they've wanted to know; my affiliates are happy because they can serve their clientele in new ways without creating a new program and make a generous commission at the same time, and I'm delighted to have intelligent students who are already well-trained in other areas of marketing and have existing businesses. Because the students are not new to entrepreneurship—just new to consulting—it's much easier for them to be successful with my program.

I've also offered exclusive high-value, interactive training in other coaching programs and masterminds simply as a relationship and lead generation tool. While the audiences for these types of sources might be significantly smaller, they often generate five to eight high-quality leads. Not bad for a single presentation to a group of 30 people!

Paid Workshops

You can also collaborate with another expert by creating a joint paid program or workshop for both of your audiences.

This is an excellent way to get an infusion of cash into your business, producing an audience you and your partner can split. However, you need to be transparent with the audience about who is a good fit for their current problems.

While this type of collaboration may involve a smaller audience, it creates an excellent yield because when people pay to participate in a program or event, they're more likely to be engaged and make future purchases. When people pay, they pay attention!

Virtual Summits

You can also collaborate by creating or participating in virtual summits. A virtual summit is an online conference in which several experts specializing in their niche speak on a broader topic. Summits are a tremendous opportunity to build an audience quickly. The experts involved have a chance to boost their visibility, build their audiences, and connect with a highly engaged audience. Although summits are a tremendous amount of work, they can be very rewarding regarding list growth.

Julia Taylor, a former intelligence officer, wanted a post-retirement line of work she could do from anywhere. She taught herself coding while traveling around the country with her husband in an RV. After growing her successful coding business, she now teaches other women coding and WordPress. Her loyal community grew organically and referred to themselves as the GeekPack. In support of her geek-themed community, she hosts an annual summit called Geekapalooza. Geekapalooza registrants receive PDF guides, geek-themed virtual backgrounds, free support in a private online group, countdown emails, quizzes, bonuses, and of course, play geek bingo.

Julia had over 6,000 participants in her most recent Geekapalooza, and the buzz associated with her summit attracted the attention of several WordPress (WP) heavy hitters, garnering an exclusive deal for attendants with WP Engine. The summit also sponsored Julia's philanthropic outreach, GeekForGeek. She partnered with Dress for Success, "a global not-for-profit organization that empowers women to achieve economic independence by providing a network of support, professional attire, and the development tools to help women thrive in work and life."[4] Julia gave these women access to her signature course, WP Rockstar.

One year, I was honored to be one of the 50 speakers Julia promoted at Geekapalooza. As a speaker, I donated a mini-course on referral marketing called "The Referral Code." My donations generated over 300 new leads for my company's email list, which turned into thousands of dollars in revenue. Whenever I meet someone interested in learning how to code, I send them Julia's way enthusiastically. Talk about a win-win!

Affiliate Partnerships (or Joint Ventures)

What's the big deal about affiliate partnerships? In 2020, Forbes reported, "When you hear 'affiliate marketing,' you may think of your favorite Instagram influencer sharing a discount for their favorite water bottle company in a post. They get a small commission on what they sell through that unique discount code if you buy it. Beyond how often it's seen on social media, though, it isn't discussed in the business realm as often as other marketing tactics, but it should be. According to Statista, affiliate marketing reached $5.4 billion in 2017 and is estimated to reach $8.2 billion by 2022. There is massive potential for affiliate partnerships to further your business's exposure and sales."[5]

Affiliate partnerships (also known as joint ventures—the terms are used interchangeably) are arrangements in which one party receives a commission in exchange for recommending a product or service. The Federal Trade Commission requires that commissions be disclosed, and that's why you often see the notice "This article includes affiliate links" on popular blogs so that consumers know that the person recommending a program or service is incentivized to do so.

The most common strategy in affiliate partnerships is to host an event—in-person or online— in which you, the person providing the program, create a custom presentation or training that promotes the services of various affiliates, with the arrangement that you receive a fee, or commission, for every sale made. Commissions range between 20 percent and 50 percent, on average.

My client Jena Castro-Casbon helps speech-language pathologists (SLPs) start, grow, and scale private practices as independent clinicians. She saw a tremendous response to traditional digital marketing channels because of her outstanding training programs. Still, we wanted to try an affiliate strategy utilizing her industry connections with other SLP influencers. Because SLPs are accustomed to open house type events in which they meet potential clients and their families, we designed an affiliate event—a virtual open house, complete with gamification and open house themed invitations—where she was able to feature former students who now have social media followings of their own. We modeled it after an open house for an academic graduate program, where graduates tell their stories. Jena provided each former student—now influencers in their own right—with a custom, trackable link to invite their followers. At the event, they highlighted the transformations and outcomes that Jena regularly achieves for her students, and the effect was much more potent than Jena posting testimonials on her website.

The event was a win-win-win for everyone involved. Hundreds of SLPs were introduced to the world of private practice. Jena's team registered dozens of new students with no up-front marketing cost, and her former students were able to earn commissions simply by inviting their audiences to a high-value educational experience. Furthermore, the SLP industry benefits because as more SLPs enter into private practice, more children and adults with speech challenges can be helped by a dedicated, caring SLP professional in a small, intimate setting. This is an excellent example of an affiliate arrangement.

The offer must be proven and established for affiliate arrangements to work well because affiliates risk their reputation with their audiences when they recommend a product. Consequently, affiliate partnerships tend to operate best at more advanced stages of entrepreneurship.

Partner Marketing

In-person partner marketing is when two businesses work together to provide additional value to their clientele by introducing companies (their partners) that offer complementary services. This type of collaboration is specific to brick-and-mortar business owners and those with a local geographic presence. Cross-promoting with a business your ideal clients already know, love, and trust enables you to reach potential clients who are more receptive to learning about your business and easier to convert into sales.

When I was consulting for The Lash Lounge, founded by my friend Anna Phillips, we developed a community marketing guide that helped local salons identify and partner with like-minded businesses that shared similar clientele to build strong community relationships, brand awareness, and credibility with future guests. One popular partnership type involved a local bridal salon and The Lash Lounge. The partnership worked because the process of buying a wedding dress is exciting, stressful, and emotional. When a bride finally says yes to a dress, she's developed trust in the people who helped her find the right one. If they recommend a service, she's going to trust that recommendation, particularly regarding something as important as their day of beauty choices. If bridal salon employees wear beautiful lashes from The Lash Lounge (through a prearranged employee program), even better! As a result, transitioning the client from the dress decision to The Lash Lounge was an easy and natural conversation.

While this example is specific to consumer services, partner marketing can work equally well for business-to-business offerings and stores specializing in product retail. Consider where else your ideal client purchases goods and services. With partner marketing, you immediately have the trust of clients that your partner refers to you. An enthusiastic referral from a trusted source carries much more weight than a well-designed marketing campaign.

BUILDING A REFERRAL PIPELINE

A referral pipeline is a tracking document to stay in touch with your best connections and partners to be top of mind when they're looking to make a referral. It's not realistic for someone you met six months ago to remember your business when a need arises. You need to stay in touch to be a top of mind reference point. Keep track of your connections and maintain contacts that have the potential to develop into referral partners.

Relationships with referral partners take time to develop; you can't expect referrals right away. Why? Because you're asking the referral partners to put their reputation on the line for you, potentially jeopardizing their relationship with their contact or client. A referral partner has to trust that you'll do a fantastic job if they send their connections your way. Asking for referrals too soon—before you've built up adequate relational capital—can be detrimental to the relationship.

A few years ago, I referred a sales rep looking for new clients to a connection from a mastermind I belong to. Several months later, my relationship reported that the sales rep had not closed a single sale; the sales rep didn't even reply to several emails asking for more information. I was horrified. Of course, I stopped referring the sales rep, but I also spent several months repairing my relationship with the mastermind colleague. Now, I limit my referral partners to an exclusive and elite list of service providers with whom I've personally had excellent experiences. Lesson learned!

If you've only had one interaction with someone, it's doubtful that they're ready to be a referral partner. Asking for referrals too soon can hurt your credibility and turn people off; it implies a lack of sophistication in your knowledge of business and relationships. But when you've had the opportunity to participate in a collaborative exchange in which you've showcased your knowledge and expertise and built trust with your partner's audience, you're on the road to gaining a referral or affiliate partner. In my experience, collaborators you stay in touch with who become part of your social media, podcast, or email community turn into referral partners. Your happiest customers turn into the best affiliate partners.

Some of the best ways to stay top of mind with your collaborators are to touch base with them at least monthly, comment on their social media, and be generous in introducing them to other valuable connections.

> **FREE RESOURCE**
>
> Want to introduce two fantastic people you know to each other? Have you met someone extraordinary, but you're unsure how to follow up with them? Visit createyourwinwin.com and get our introduction scripts. They'll give you the exact words you need to follow up with your most recent connection.

THINKING CREATIVELY ABOUT COLLABORATIONS

There are many more profound ways to collaborate beyond the obvious. Some collaborators end up co-creating more meaningful or long term, like Gino and Rob (see chapter 2). Someone who was originally a great colleague or friend may become an even better business partner down the road.

> **PRO TIP**
>
> Authentic outreach gets genuine replies. Sometimes, a potential collaborator will turn down a proposal. They may not feel like they know you well enough. Ensure you're committed to bringing value to a potential collaborator by establishing credibility, being in their audience, having the right intention, and building a long-term relationship. As you move forward as part of their community, their "No" will often become a "Yes."
>
> For example, here's the script I recently used to ask an influencer with a million Instagram followers to be on my podcast (and it worked!).

> "Hi, ___ and team! I was just catching up on podcasts and noticed you're on tour to promote your new book on business growth. You're on the podcast of several mutual friends, including Mel and Stacy. Would you like to come to mine? It might be interesting to talk about personal development as it relates to growing a business, and I haven't heard you discuss that angle yet. Either way, wishing you tons of love and blessings with your book!"
>
> - If you break down my message, you can see the following:
> - I established credibility by sharing whom we had in common.
> - I offered a unique angle that provided new value to the marketplace.
> - I played it cool so the influencer wouldn't feel like I was just a taker (in truth, I was genuinely curious about her to take on that angle, and I figured my audience would be too!)
>
> When reaching out, think about how you can be an asset to your connection and their audience, and work from that intention.

When seeking out collaborations, remember to be open. As you connect with others, there may be a way to collaborate that goes beyond the obvious. To develop a collaboration, look for gaps in what your potential partner covers for their audience. For example, after looking into their community, you may realize that you have insight, experience, or a story that their audience would love. If the topic has already been covered, it's unlikely that the potential collaborator will be motivated to feature you.

Finally, don't discount small audiences. In this book, I'm intentionally sharing examples from those with larger companies and followings *and* examples from experts who are lesser known and have smaller audiences. Why? Because there's a massive power in small audiences. It's challenging to maintain that power as you gain audience members. Small communities and audiences tend to have more engagement, excitement, and trust. Don't assume you need to collaborate with someone with a large audience to succeed. Regarding partnerships, quality wins over quantity every day of the week.

After any connection—whether in a group or one-on-one—it's a good practice to set aside time for a follow-up. If it's appropriate, at the end of a connection, see if you can come up with a win-win idea for sharing with one another's audiences. Suppose you have complementary audiences or offers, brainstorm ways to be on each other's platforms, or create a more formal collaboration. If the conversation goes in that direction, follow up with a call or next touch point so that you can start making plans or introductions to the appropriate people.

Keep in mind that the goal of every new connection or interaction is not to make a sale or enroll someone into your program but to find a creative way to collaborate. When you collaborate with new connections, you get to know each other well, and you can establish credibility with each other. The casual conversation only reveals so much about an individual; the truth comes out (good or bad) about the quality of a business' offering only once you start collaborating.

Remember that the goal of any interaction is to establish credibility. Suppose you're feeling overwhelmed by the idea of making a large volume of connections to make this system work in your business. In that case, you can build yourself up as a credible expert and establish a fantastic reputation by going deeper with fewer people. Over time, you'll become a solid, reasonable superconnector living in a world of cold outreach attempts and too much reliance on unpredictable social media algorithms.

THE STAYING POWER OF RELATIONSHIPS

Brands can build trust more quickly by leveraging relationships than any other type of marketing activity. Relationship marketing allows you to stand out as a leader in your industry in a way few other investments can. The more known you are, the more powerful you are. Connections with new audiences are fast-tracked, allowing you to grow your visibility further. It's challenging to get new clients willing to pay a premium for your products and services when you're unknown. That's why consistently creating collaborations results in new leads and sales. It makes you more visible and known. Your ultimate goal in collaborating with others is to build an expert brand and help people understand the value of your services.

How do you go about making connections and creating win-win situations in a way that maximizes your time? How do you find these magical connections that I've been describing?

- First, make the decision to commit to relationship marketing. When trying to succeed at many marketing activities as a scaling organization, small business, or solopreneur, it's natural to feel frustrated, overwhelmed, and burned out. By making that decision, it helps to focus your offer.
- Participate in at least three different communities, where you can actively seek win-win relationships and get yourself in front of new referral partners and collaborators. If you're not sure which ones to join, begin attending trial events or open houses for various organizations and take into consideration where ideal partners for your business would congregate.
- Dedicate time every week to relationship marketing to follow up with your contacts and stay top of mind. If you see something new happening for them, such as an award or new partnership posted online, send them a message of congratulations.

> *Your* **RELATIONSHIPS & REPUTATION** *are your two most valuable assets — as an — entrepreneur.*
>
> — Laura Meyer

Your relationships and reputation are your most valuable assets as an entrepreneur. If you want to kick-start the growth of your business, you need to develop these two areas more deeply. Relationships and reputation are like an invisible hand that pushes your company ahead and enhances all your direct response marketing efforts.

I recommend participating in at least three live events or organizations a year so that you have ample opportunities to bring your connections to new communities and create new opportunities for the people you're meeting. This will help you grow your relationships and reputation. It also allows you to keep building your audience and creating your platform; you'll have something to offer in exchange when you meet a strong potential collaboration partner. You wouldn't go to a dinner party bearing only a single can of Diet Coke (side note: if you come to my house, I love a good charcuterie board); in the same way, you need to bring something valuable to exchange with your connections. If you have a niche offer or a unique audience for which you solve a specific problem, seek connections who solve similar problems. When you ask for specific introductions and know what kind of connections you're looking for, you'll make great connections instead of simply being caught up in friendly chitchat. Although being friendly has merit, making business connections should be your highest priority in reading this book.

WHEN EXPERT OFFERS MESH

When I first saw Lena's work in a community we belong to, I knew I needed her to help me uplevel my branding. As we worked together, I realized she uses brand strategy correctly—to tell a brand story and convey emotion. I had been providing a mini version of this service as part of my signature package for my clients, and the designs I provided were good. But Lena's design work had bespoke beauty that's hard to find!

We complement each other so well. I serve women by helping them develop businesses that will grow organically through authentic interactions with their markets. Lena allows women to create robust brand strategies that share more who they are with their ideal clients. It's a match made in business heaven!

I wanted every one of my clients to be in love with their branding because that boosts their confidence as they present themselves to their markets. And I'm all about helping them grow their business confidence and helping them feel like they know what they're doing! I approached Lena for a joint-venture opportunity in which I would take care of strategy and remain client facing. She would take what I developed with the client and turn it into a beautiful and communicative visual package. She agreed! She has saved me 4–6 hours of work per client and always produces logos and color palettes more beautifully than I could imagine.

I know my service is valuable beyond what I can provide alone, and we've become business besties! I can offer my clients a unique and high-quality branding service, and Lena gets compensated for each of the sales! She enjoys being able to support women in the early stage of business without having to do all the strategy and brand education.

We've become great referral resources for each other because we have a strong understanding of the value each of our services provides. We also meet frequently to cowork in our businesses. She helps me ensure my visual brand strategy stays on track, and I help her refine her copywriting and get unstuck when she's developing something new in her business. We love to cheer each other on and support in any way we can!

—Danielle Mendoza, Be Myself Now

Danielle's story is an example of a simple connection growing into a working relationship and referral partnership. In your communities, be active in regular social events designed for connecting. If you're part of a social media group or a private platform where a community is hosted, take the time to do a keyword search on the type of person you're looking to meet. If someone introduces herself in a way that complements your business, you can follow up and say, "Your introduction looks great. I think we might be able to collaborate," and explain why. Let them know that you notice their hard work and that you're appreciative of it.

If you read an article about your industry, category, or field written by someone else in your area or local geography, reach out to the author and let them know how much you appreciate their work. They'll be grateful, and you'll leave a lasting positive impression. Doing your research and customizing your approaches will go a long way in a world where most outreach is clearly automated and horrifyingly impersonal.

Great relationships don't happen overnight. They're built on trust, communication, and constant nurturing. At the same time, partnerships with the right people should feel natural and inspiring.

When reaching out, be open, honest, confident, and authentic. Identify your shared goals and values, and let your conversations build on that mutual foundation. You'll know when you've partnered with the right person because you'll both be energized and excited to move forward.

> **FREE RESOURCE**
>
> Visit createyourwinwin.com and get our 10 (non-spammy) messages to send to potential collaborators and partners. They're the perfect resource when you need the right words to make a genuine connection.

CHAPTER SUMMARY

To develop win-win relationships, we need to change how we think about new connections. Most new connections are more often someone that you can collaborate with than your ideal client. Once you've reframed your view of new connections so that you see them as potential collaborators rather than potential clients or friendly conversations, you'll be able to take advantage of the collaboration ideas and tips presented in this chapter.

CHAPTER 5

IMPLEMENTING THE WIN-WIN

When I moved my career path from traditional brick-and-mortar to online business consulting and was seeking to build my clientele as a new expert in a highly competitive space, I created lead magnets, ran paid traffic ads, and wrote and rewrote my LinkedIn profile more times than I can even count.

During that time, I built an expensive, time-consuming sales funnel to build my email list based on a coaching program I heavily invested in. I grew frustrated by the amount of time and money I was spending on marketing and the lack of return I saw, but I kept plugging along.

One day my former attorney, Charles, sent me an email: "Laura, I see what you're doing online, and I love it. I think you're born for this, and you're so good at it. You've always been a genius when it comes to marketing and branding. I'd love for you to speak in front of our audience."

I politely dismissed his kind offer because I was busy with my ongoing list of marketing tasks: "Charles, thanks so much. I'm good. I'm working on this big project right now."

He replied, "No, I really want you to help my audience. Will you please do this webinar for me?"

I agreed but treated it like I was doing Charles a favor.

Little did I know.

It was much fun. We laughed together as I shared stories and client examples. He was so affirming, and it was clear to his audience how much he trusted, admired, and believed in me as a marketer.

After the webinar, Charles posted the training to his LinkedIn and blog and shared it with his email list (Charles is a marketing-savvy, entrepreneurial attorney). About a year later, I analyzed where my business had come from over the last 12 months as part of an annual business analysis exercise. As I looked at the different lead sources, I realized that half of my business in my first year as a consultant, about $70,000, had come from that one webinar.

What was happening?!

Reflecting upon this year later, there were many reasons why this webinar worked. I had an excellent reputation and preexisting credibility with Charles, which permeated the interview. *He* thought highly of me and trusted me, and the audience saw it. Because the content I taught was congruent with the core offer of my consulting company, the leads generated from that presentation were a natural fit for our services. As a result, all of the leads generated from that one activity became consulting clients with a 100 percent close rate.

While I love a complex sales funnel and advise my clients on how to optimize them regularly, it's not always the *most* effective approach to growing your business. I'm not saying that your next collaboration will turn into $70,000 in revenue, but I *am* saying that sometimes we spin in circles, trying to figure something out when the answer is so simple that we just can't even see it.

As I mentioned, we often underestimate the people we're already connected to. There are potential win-win opportunities within your existing network waiting to be discovered. The deeper your relationship and the more credibility you have with a connection (and the more credibility they have with you), the more effective the collaboration. And like my situation with Charles, your next referral partner is probably someone you're already connected to—a former vendor, partner, colleague, co-worker, or client.

> **PRO TIP**
>
> If you haven't done so already, go through your LinkedIn or Facebook friend list and write down the people you're connected to and their current roles. Think creatively about whether you could establish a win-win partnership with each contact. Someone you already have a strong connection with can be your next collaborator.

Your next win-win may simply be opportunities for collaboration and increased visibility. It may be mentoring people or guesting on other experts' platforms. It may be growing your brand or simply feeling a little less alone on your entrepreneurial journey. Regardless of the outcome, knowing what you want from a win-win collaboration is essential. Remember that trust is either built or broken in collaborating with other experts. If you create value during a partnership, it's possible that they'll be so impressed with you that they end up hiring you; this has happened to me on multiple occasions. But your credibility is at stake if you're disorganized or have to reschedule numerous times, or worse, you don't show up.

When setting up win-win collaborations, the number one goal should be credibility and visibility—not appearing hungry for new business. Credibility and visibility create leads and referrals, and it's essential to trust that the collaboration process will grow your business. Before high-quality leads and referrals come, we must do the work of establishing credibility and becoming visible. You may collaborate with someone every now and then, and they immediately realize that you have the solution they've been looking for. That's wonderful, but it's also rare. What usually happens is that trust, credibility, and visibility build over time, and qualified leads and referrals come slowly as a result.

In collaborations, seek to build credibility and help other people understand the value of your services. With every communication with other experts, you're building your reputation.

COMMITMENTS MATTER

Most people know the importance of being prepared, showing up on time, and researching. Still, I'm often surprised by how many last-minute reschedules and no-shows I encounter, even with established entrepreneurs. One former client who came to me to grow her struggling membership had a nice-sized social media following but was a habitual over-promiser. The two issues were very much related. She off-boarded as soon as she signed on as a client, not because she wasn't talented at her craft but because she consistently overpromised and then struggled to meet her commitments. Of course, there are always things beyond our control, but there's also a professional way to handle promises you cannot keep.

If you have a family emergency, communicate that you're in a challenging situation, that you care about the connection you've established, and that you can't follow through on the previously scheduled commitment because of a problem beyond your control. If you communicate in this way, you'll protect your reputation and save your connection. People will want to work with you if you have a good reputation as someone who keeps commitments. Imagine you're constantly running late to meetings, appearing confused, looking frantic or overscheduled, or cancelling at the last minute and being chased down to get what you promised them. In that case, people will hesitate to collaborate with you or refer business. We all have bad days but do your best to keep your business persona *consistent*. I think one of the first hires every visionary business owner should make if they're feeling overwhelmed is an executive assistant. That way, you can ensure that you show up at your best when it's time to make new connections.

Another obstacle to success in creating win-win partnerships is imposter syndrome. If presenting to new audiences or partnering with companies is leading to stress or overwhelm for you, please know it's not uncommon to feel uncomfortable about guesting on other people's platforms. You may wonder, "Who am I to claim this expertise or market position when so many other people are good at what I do?" If you're struggling with this, I want to encourage you to adopt a new way of thinking. Others may do what you do, but only you have lived your story and brought your unique perspective and experience; that will attract ideal clients. The more authentic you are, the more valuable your perspective will be. Collaborating initiates a compounding effect that gives you access to new clients because best-fit customers in new audiences will feel a bond with you based on the unique attributes of your organization.

DELIVERING GREAT INTERVIEWS

You've done it! You've scheduled a collaboration, shown up on time, tested your microphone, provided your noisy Labradoodle with something to do other than bark at the squirrels outside your office, silenced your phone, and you're ready to go!

> Win-Win partnerships give us the opportunity to move faster, together.
>
> — *Laura Meyer*

So, what do you talk about? How can you make a long-term impression? How can you target those in the audience who would be the best people for you to work with?

Before your interview begins, it's a good idea to do some studying. Pull up the host's blog or podcast, look at what's already been covered, and come prepared with a unique angle that hasn't been discussed yet. By doing this, you add a refreshing perspective and create additional value. Many times, topics are agreed upon before an interview, but doing your homework adds an extra dimension of preparedness that will elevate the quality of the discussion.

A partner interview aims to deliver your area of genius, educate the market, help people understand what makes your perspective unique, and gives people a taste of what it's like to work with your company. If you do this well, you'll be positioned as a thought leader on that particular topic and start to become known as someone who offers high-quality programs and services. Never take an interview opportunity as an avenue for self-promotion. People quickly recognize when you're only out to get the next dollar in the door. The more sophisticated your ideal client is, the easier it is for them to spot inauthenticity and choose not to work with you. I've conducted interviews for my podcast that I decided not to publish because the entire interview was a boring sales fest. Creating value should be your top priority.

You can start an interview by sharing the origin story of your business in 5–10 minutes at the most. Your business likely began from an aha moment in which you realized that your product or service was something that could make a difference for others.

Your values—what you believe in, who you are, and what you know through experience— should be embedded in your origin story. Leave out extraneous information that doesn't apply to your offer.

I've found that my consulting clients usually have a variety of decisive moments that shape their lives and businesses. But as we dig further, only one or two stories typically connect to their offer. The more aligned your story is with your offer, the more often an interview will produce new leads for your brand.

> **PRO TIP**
>
> Communicating an authentic origin story creates psychological alignment with ideal clients and collaborators because they have the same values as you. Starting with your origin story allows you to speak deeply about your values, mission, vision, and the *why* behind your business. As you provide your perspective on your work, share specific stories about your clients and experiences and describe how those stories tie into your core offer.

As you move beyond your origin story, it's helpful to have two or three talking points—things that may conflict with conventional wisdom in your niche—and speak specifically about client examples or stories that illustrate your point. The goal is to create an interview based on your unique story, values, and insightful moments of reference that can build your reputation; this helps you become more and more known. The more polarizing or unusual your viewpoint, the more you will attract your ideal client with a lighthouse marketing strategy (see chapter 2).

As an interview wraps up, share a compelling call to action that gives the audience specific next steps for working with you.

PROVIDE FREE TRAINING

Providing free training inside a mastermind, event, or paid program is slightly different from giving a complimentary interview to the public. Although both are designed to create value, I provide a set of regular speaking topics as options when I'm booked on a podcast or a collaborator's platform. I'm much more amenable to customize training content for a paid program. Because developing custom content is more labor intensive, I only do it when I know there's a significant opportunity to generate leads or traffic to my business.

For example, I'm a guest speaker in Master Coach Kris Plachy's How to CEO program, a leadership training program that helps female entrepreneurs become assertive, confident, and effective leaders. The custom content I create for her program teaches how to make your first full marketing hire in a high-growth business. Suppose a female entrepreneur is investing in leadership training. In that case, she's either leading a team that includes marketing professionals or looking to hire one, and she needs a growth consultant. This speaking opportunity, which requires just an hour of my time a few times a year is a fantastic lead generator for my consulting business. The win-win is that Kris can deliver valuable information in her program that's outside her specific expertise, and I can establish visibility and credibility with a small group of ideal consulting clients.

What's the difference between a keynote talk you provide for a fee and free training inside a collaborator's paid program? Ultimately, it's up to you to decide. If you're a trained professional speaker, you're already familiar with a stage talk's fee structure and delivery. In complementary trainings, it's very appropriate to present a call to action at the end. If you're a paid speaker, it's usually not appropriate. The compensation you receive replaces the opportunity for business development activities at the end of your talk.

A COMPELLING CALL TO ACTION

The call to action at the end of a speaking opportunity is short compared to the rest of your talk, but it's the most critical segment because your call to action is the part of your talk that will result in

> *Make Gratitude & gifting a habitual part of your Win-Win collaborations.*
>
> ♡
>
> — Laura Meyer

new leads for your company. Sometimes simply directing people to your website or preferred platform is highly effective; it may be the only thing you need to do to establish a win-win collaboration that grows your business. Your goal should be consistency in guesting on other platforms and communicating your call to action. One collaboration a week over 52 weeks can turn into hundreds of qualified leads. Consistent visibility and a compelling call to action pays off.

What are some effective calls to action? Offer an e-book or a piece of gated content, like a lead magnet, that's congruent with your speaking topic and offer. Gated content requires people to provide you with their contact information in exchange for a free resource (much like the free resources made available in this book). The free content you provide should bridge the topic you spoke about and the product or services you sell.

It should provide an easy way for people to learn more about you and get on your email list.

> **📢 PRO TIP**
>
> Creating a vanity URL makes it much easier for people to contact you than a link that includes numbers, letters, and multiple forward slashes. For example, scalewithjoy.com is a vanity URL that I use as a call to action when I'm speaking on stages or podcasts where my ideal consulting client would hear it; it's much better than a long web address that's hard to remember. A virtual assistant or a technology support specialist can easily create a link and set it up to forward to any page on your website.

If you don't have a lead magnet or don't have time to create one, that's okay. All you need is a platform where people can connect with you. You might say, "I love answering questions about this topic, and if you have any questions or would like to share your experience, fill out the form on my website." If this is your chosen call to action, ensure you give people a straightforward way to contact you. If you think a question is a little bit off-topic or more than you can cover in the interview, that's an excellent opportunity to direct people to your content online or in your program. You could say, "In my program, I have a full guide for this question and cover it in more detail." Make it clear that you have a program that can help. This creates an opening for people to contact you down the road.

Suppose you have a high-ticket, one-to-one offers like professional services, coaching, or consulting services. In that case, you'll want to invite listeners into a sales conversation with you or your sales team. If you have a one-to-many offer, such as a membership, live event, course, or retail, you'll want to use a lead magnet to build your email list, as that's typically the best way to market volume offers.

Ideally, you should have two or three pieces of gated content or lead magnets that invite your ideal clients to become part of your email list. Depending on the topic of an interview, choose the lead magnet that will create the most value for the audience. Then create a welcome sequence—three to five emails sent automatically to subscribers once they opt-in to your lead magnet. The goal of the welcome series is to begin a relationship with each new subscriber and allow them to reply or click on a valuable offer within the sequence. This increases the open rate for future emails and sales opportunities the next time you open enrollment for your paid programs.

CARRYING THE WIN TO COMPLETION

When you get an introduction or a referral, even the smallest gesture of gratitude goes a long way. My assistant sends a token of appreciation in the form of a $10 Starbucks gift card after every podcast interview or guest appearance. It's a small gesture, but the number of messages and texts I receive from that thank-you gift shows that the little things count. What matters most is that people hear from you.

I make gratitude and gifting a habitual part of win-win collaborations. It's a meaningful way to make people think of you the next time they have an opportunity. Sending gift cards or flowers goes a long way in a world where many overlook the importance of gratitude. Behavioral psychologist Dan Ariely writes, "As for gratitude, saying thanks has a magic effect on the giver, so don't sweat the exact method of saying thanks too much, and just say it a few times."[1] What matters is that we say thanks; how we say it matters less. Send someone flowers, give them a gift card, a call, or a singing telegram. It all works as long as you remember to follow up and say thanks.

CHAPTER SUMMARY

In any collaborative relationship, the goal is to develop a trusted, expert brand. We do this by conducting ourselves professionally and doing our homework so that we always bring value to our guest appearances on other people's platforms and present our values and beliefs. If we're constantly visible through our collaborations and give people a clear call to action, we'll reap the rewards in new business. Participating in collaborations is one of the most valuable marketing activities you can prioritize for your business, whether to grow your list or increase the frequency of sales conversations.

CHAPTER 6

BUILDING COMMUNITY

The final step in the win-win formula is to engage in and develop a community among your ideal clients, audiences, and peers to stay visible and top of mind in your industry. We started with credibility, which builds your reputation in the marketplace and motivates others to partner with you. As you use credibility to increase the visibility of your organization, new audiences, leads, and customers will start pouring into your ecosystem. From there, you want to start building community with your audience and customers to keep the momentum going. The result? Saying goodbye to all the complicated noise online and trading it for the magic of human connection.

For many of us, the Covid-19 pandemic changed our priorities related to our need for community. We've started to think about whom we want to associate with from a new perspective. Many of us have deepened our beliefs, philosophies, or spiritual commitments. We have a renewed sense of purpose; we want to leave a legacy. There was a sense of impermanence in the significant shifts that took place in humanity over the two years of the pandemic.

Win-Win Formula

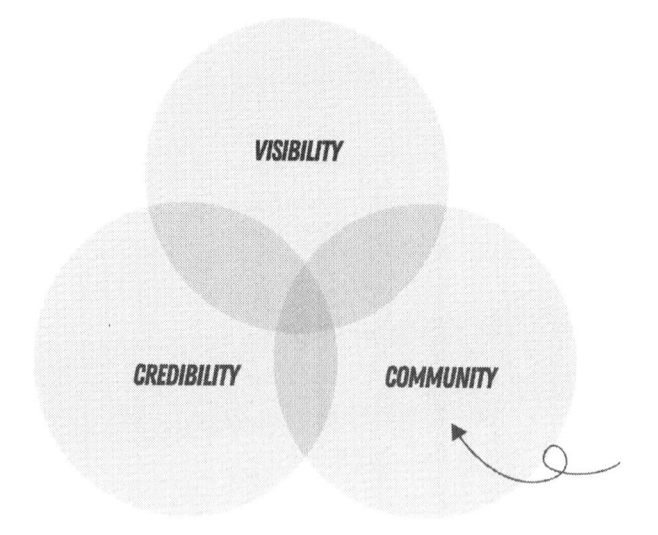

VISIBILITY

CREDIBILITY **COMMUNITY**

At the most recent school open house for my children, one of my children's teachers stated that she had only gathered enough teaching material during the pandemic to be out of the classroom for two weeks, not two years. As a collective humanity, we were required to move from a state of shock to acceptance in a short period of time. As reality started to set in, different emotions took hold. We began to realize the loss and struggle we would need to endure. But then when the world started to open again, something lifted, and we realized that what gives our lives meaning is not being busy all day long; what defines the quality of our lives is the community we share, how much the people in our communities can trust us, and how united we are to them. For many of us, the circle we went into the pandemic with is not the one we want to maintain going forward;

we need something different in our personal or professional lives. If you're feeling this emptiness—a sense of not knowing what to do next, a lack of purpose, or loneliness—what you might be missing is community.

Before the pandemic, life moved so fast that many people didn't have the time to reflect. During the pandemic, many people experienced deep transformations, often, transformations of purpose. Many have embarked on healing journeys to recover from the loss and stress of living through a pandemic. Life has become more delicate. People are measuring the quality of their lives, the goals they set, and the outcomes they want to achieve, not just in terms of dollars and cents but in terms of how their relationships make them feel about their life experiences.

What gives us a sense of purpose is no longer just being busy. We now ask whether there's something meaningful behind what we're doing. We often consider how we spend our time and energy and the people we spend them with. Sitting in the social circles at the country club or preschool pickup, many think, "Gosh, why do I feel so alone when there are so many people around me?" It's a very confusing feeling, and we scarcely know how to process it.

Community is critical; it can even extend our lives. Scientists have identified five blue zones[1] around the world, areas that have the highest concentrations of centenarians compared to the rest of the world. Studies have found that, yes, they have plant-based diets primarily; and yes, they exercise and garden. But the primary reason they live longer, happier, and healthier lives is because of community. That is the life-changing power of being with people who share your beliefs and values.

When we exchange ideas, encouragement, advice, experience, and resources with others through community, it keeps us from sitting on the sidelines. It gets us into the arena. When that happens, we start taking action that we wouldn't have otherwise because we no longer try to climb the mountain alone. We have others who can help us process any problem we're working on. This further develops trust, and then business growth happens naturally. This takes place even though that isn't the primary intention; the intention is community.

When we enter a community mindset, we find that much of the value we receive comes simply from the sharing of experiences, either one-on-one or speaking in groups. When we become part of a community or enter into the community of others, we learn from the experiences of others and share our experiences with them; this is the primary way we feel seen, heard, and valued.

When we share our experiences through collaborations, both parties benefit because our partners can listen to our experiences and take away the pieces that apply to them. As I was writing this chapter while having my morning coffee, I received a message from a friend I hadn't heard from in a while. She said, "I've been thinking of you every day for the last six months. And I'm finally reaching out because I'm at a breaking point, and I know you can help me."

Knowing the fragile place she was in, I simply shared my experience, telling her not what she should do but my thinking when I was in her shoes and the outcomes of my decisions. I walked her through my decision-making process, which created much more value for her than if I had simply told her what to do. When she replied, she was relieved and uplifted. I was so grateful that my experience was given more meaning by helping her make the best decision for her business. Although everyone has opinions, experienced experts are pros at sharing their journey with others in ways that build trust, credibility, and community.

Although everyone has opinions, experienced experts are pros at sharing their journey with others in ways that build trust, credibility, and community.

BUILDING YOUR COMMUNITY

As your visibility grows and you share your thoughts with the world, your audience will also increase. Over time, readers of your emails or blog and your podcast listeners become members of your community. As you build your email list from those you attract into your business through compelling content, follow up with high-value emails each week. If you produce weekly podcasts, you can hire a writer to listen to the podcast and send a nurture email summary out to your email list. When you engage with subscribers and audience members, you naturally build a community through the types of interactions we've covered in previous chapters. Audience members may not buy from you (most won't), but they'll listen to your podcast, read your books, follow you on social media and validate your paid offers simply because they're consuming your material. As your credibility and visibility grow, the ideal clients hanging out on your email list or your podcast audience will come forward to work with your organization. You'll be surprised by how many ideal clients are waiting in the wings of your subscriber list, only to jump at the opportunity to work together given the right message.

Timing is critical in purchasing decisions. The day someone subscribes to your email list is most often not the day they're ready to buy from you. According to an article published by Salesforce, "[I]t takes 6–8 marketing touches to generate a viable sales lead.... The six to eight touches it takes to qualify a lead are crucial components of the lead nurturing process, allowing marketing the opportunity to educate and inform prospects as they move through each stage in the buying journey."[2] Developing relationships and engaging with your audience—your community—is a non-sales, feel-good way to follow up with prospects continually.

You don't need to have a paid offering such as a membership to develop community. Community building can occur on your social media account, with your email list, in private groups, or with your podcast listenership. Community can be formal (paid memberships and programs) or informal (connecting with a listener who started following you after hearing your guest's appearance on a podcast). While developing community as part of a paid program is vital for developing a peer-to-peer support system, community creation starts with you. The best businesses start with a movement of people who have shared beliefs before the money is exchanged.

My dear friend Shana Bresnahan is a community consultant who works with some of the world's top membership site owners and paid communities. Her signature framework, Community Cultivated™, teaches business owners how to create a sense of belonging in their communities. The four pillars of community—cause, culture, communication, and connection—are what attract people into communities and keep them coming back for more. Shana says that if you want a thriving online community, your community members need to feel like they're a part of something bigger than themselves.

Community building goes beyond tactics and strategies. When done well, it taps into the psychology of human nature. When we connect with our communities, we make them feel understood, safe, and seen. These feelings are an essential part of feeling connected. Shana says that when people feel connected, they stay longer and show up more fully in the world. When you focus on creating a community—not just an audience— your business and impact will grow exponentially.

> **🔊 PRO TIP**
>
> Engagement is a key metric to measure to ascertain how well you're developing your community. Engagement goes beyond consumption and gauges how community members interact with you and each other. Engagement can be measured in various ways, depending on the platform. Click, response, and reply rates indicate how well your emails engage your community, but strong open and click rates show how interesting your content is to the community. For social media, track post engagement rates, and for podcasts, track reviews and downloads. Keep track of these metrics relative to benchmarks you set for your own company. The trends you see from month to month are a good indicator of how well your communication engages your community.

PARTICIPATING IN OTHER COMMUNITIES

Ali Brown, a business coach and client who specializes in helping women entrepreneurs, has created leading-edge entrepreneurial programs for over 15 years, building her company to Inc. 500 rankings, multimillion dollar revenues, and international recognition. She's the creator and host of the acclaimed *Glambition*® Radio podcast and has served as an entrepreneur delegate for the United Nations Foundation's Global Accelerator.

Despite her accumulated accolades, Ali grew tired of going into rooms full of men to meet other entrepreneurs at an advanced business level. Ali developed a community called The Trust that specifically serves women-owned businesses earning $1 million plus—a grossly underserved group, particularly in curated networks and programming.

> *Experienced experts are pros at sharing* **THEIR JOURNEY** *with others in ways that build trust, credibility & community.*
>
> — Laura Meyer

Having been a part of masterminds dominated by men, Ali found that women had different conversations when only women were in the room. Now that Ali created this safe space for women entrepreneurs to come together, The Trust community has taken on a life of its own, and many ideas have blossomed out of their collective consciousness. Strong standards for a community exclusively for women ensures a unique dynamic—it fosters elevated discussions, shared strategies, and referred contacts. Within The Trust's first year, members launched companies together, created joint ventures, closed six- and seven-figure deals, made real estate investments, shared valuable private resources, and supported each other's professional and personal missions.

When searching for a community, it's essential to keep in mind that not every community is ideal for you. You may have read the description of The Trust and felt that it didn't sound right to you, perhaps because it's not for the beginning stages of entrepreneurship or because it's specifically for women. By contrast, you may have been attracted to The Trust's closed-door gatherings that are designed for conversations about a bigger game of business. You might connect with one community and realize that a different one is the right fit. It's essential to be part of a community that operates under a philosophy that matches your values to spend time with the right people in the right way. Otherwise, a community may end up being just another thing on your calendar and a waste of time rather than something that changes your life.

The events and programs in a community should be designed for reciprocity and include your peers in business and life. When we build trust in community with others, we become someone who people want to stay connected to, someone they want to introduce to clients and be friends with. These connections result in an ecosystem fueled by relationships and generate the most significant business growth.

A WIN-WIN COLLABORATION

Early in 2022, I hosted a Q&A session for folks who had questions about the TEDx process. The same week, vocal empowerment guide Brienne Hennessy hosted her own workshop. A fellow member of a networking group we were in attended both of our sessions, and afterward, she encouraged Brienne and me to consider creating something together. She saw the potential for a highly aligned, synergistic collaboration that could significantly impact our audiences. With that nudge, Brienne and I scheduled time to brainstorm potential opportunities for collaboration, and together, we created a workshop titled "Press Play on TEDx: Giving Voice to Your Idea Worth Spreading." The half-day seminar helped students refine their "idea worth spreading" and provided vocal exercises and activities to strengthen the physical and verbal representation of their ideas. The goal was for all participants to be ready to apply for TEDx events by the end of the workshop.

As a TEDx coach, I help my clients define their message, create their talk, and deliver it impactfully. Brienne's specialty is voice, which is an essential part of delivery! Moreover, Brienne focuses on helping clients connect their inner voice—intuition, values, and self—to their physical voice. It made so much sense for us to partner so that our students could determine the message they wanted to share in their TEDx talks and learn how to use their inner and physical voices to support their ideas.

Our businesses are rooted in our belief that we all have an idea to share and that that idea comes from something inside us—what Brienne refers to as our inner voice. Our businesses help others express the ideas that come from deep within them.

We each approach that concept differently, so working together gave our students a well-rounded approach!

It was important for Brienne and me to work with clients and collaborators whose values aligned with ours, so we both felt the green light as we got to know each other better through our initial talks about the possibility of collaboration.

We connected with each other's audiences through our collaboration, expanding our reach. Because we've both developed relationships with other business owners in our networking group, several fellow members also spontaneously shared our event, putting us in front of even more new audiences. Through the workshop itself, we developed leads for our broader programs too.

In the collaboration process, Brienne and I learned more about each other's services, shared ideas, gained new perspectives on each other's educational content, created exponential value for our students, and grew our audience awareness by highlighting each other's work in our emails and on social media.

We had a handful of folks ask us if we'd be teaching our workshop again, and we decided that yes, we would! We plan to offer the workshop quarterly to continue sharing our audiences and generating leads for our main programs. We've also discussed other ways to collaborate. For example, in 2023, I plan to open a group TEDx coaching program and invite Brienne to present as a specialty coach within that program.

—Cathlyn Melvin, TEDx Coach + Copywriter

SELLING TO YOUR COMMUNITY

Many entrepreneurs, even experienced ones with large audiences, are hesitant to directly sell to communities they've developed through platform exchanges, speaking opportunities, and the visibility strategies outlined in previous chapters. Perhaps they feel as though they're violating an unwritten code by selling too much or too often to their audience—people who listened to them speak simply to get more information. If this is you, I want to share something with you that may help you approach this business area differently.

If you have an offer that can genuinely help the people you're selling to and can make their lives or businesses better, you have an obligation to let them know about it. The average email open rate is around 20 percent, so most people aren't going to see what you offer if you only put it in front of them once. But at the same time, you don't want to frequently send a direct-buy email to your audience. What should you do instead? I recommend creating regular, high-value bridges that move your audience from passively consuming content to opting into a more intimate setting. These bridges take the following forms:

- Free masterclasses or webinars
- Complimentary pieces of training or coaching sessions
- Paid workshops that last anywhere from a few hours to several days
- Complimentary strategy sessions
- A paid power hour that allows registrants to pick your brain on an issue or get a solution to a common problem
- Inexpensive live events at desirable locations

These bridges create value for your prospects; even if they attend and leave without purchasing anything, they'll feel they were served well and received good value for their money and time. You want them to leave thinking, "If the free or inexpensive material is like this, the paid programs must be incredible!"

With bridge products, you're selling something so high value that you can't help but think that anyone who doesn't take you up on your offer must be out to lunch.

> **PRO TIP**
>
> For inbound sales conversations, I love to use a software called VideoAsk. It allows me to place a small video on a sales page, inside a weekly nurture email, or on the confirmation page of an opt-in. The videos immediately engage my audience in two-way communication. We even use VideoAsk to collect our students' net promoter score (NPS, a standard measure of customer satisfaction). VideoAsk is a great way to increase intimacy with prospects if you don't have a sales team but want to add a human touch to your sales process.

Another example of a bridge product is a $37 mini-workshop I created called The Referral Code. Eventually, I turned it into a stand-alone on-demand mini-course. The referral code is a fantastic value for the price; thousands of purchasers have used it over the last few years. The workshop gives potential clients a taste of what it's like to work with me and the type of value they can expect from my paid programs at just a fraction of the investment they'd need to make to work with my team directly. Many have gone on to invest in other products and services.

A consulting client, Patty Palmer, is the founder and CEO of Deep Space Sparkle, an art education company that provides busy art teachers with a done-for-you art school curriculum and supporting resources through a membership program, The Sparkler's Club. As a bridge product, Patty and her team offer art teachers free training geared toward helping them transition from being overworked, underappreciated, and often underpaid to thriving art teachers. Because this transformation is a giant leap for much of her audience, Patty's pieces of training are available at no charge so that she can help as many art teachers as possible, regardless of whether they join her paid programs. Although Patty could easily justify selling her high-quality trainings to her audience, offering the trainings at no charge gives her the best chance to develop new relationships with as many art teachers as possible.

Whether you offer free or paid bridge products is a personal decision. Consider most of your ideal client's situation when they join your community. Which type of bridge product would work better? Paid bridge products tend to generate fewer participants, but they convert at a higher rate because participants have already decided to invest with you. Free bridge products tend to create more participants but convert at a lower rate. Finding the best option for your business is an exercise in considering your ideal customer, price point, sales process, and the overall lifetime value of your average customer.

COMMUNITY OVER COMPETITION: THE RIGHT MINDSET FOR BUILDING COMMUNITY

Some common mindset issues can get in the way of utilizing relationship marketing to grow your business. The mindset needed for relationship marketing differs from that required for any other marketing effort. In many ways, mindset is crucial in making relationship marketing work.

Many people avoid communities because they feel it's safer to automate and stay emotionally distanced from their marketing and sales processes. But connection and community are the factors that are genuinely effective in growing businesses. To increase your income and impact, you have to be willing to increase the intimacy of your offer by entering into community. Build your own community and bravely enter into other communities. Then you'll generate new collaboration partners with whom you can build credibility and visibility.

Building community involves putting yourself out there, and you might feel like you're not enough or worry about what people will say about you. As a defense mechanism, many people retreat into focusing on too many things at once. When you embrace community, you move past that defense mechanism, provide support for others, and allow yourself to be supported. Community affirms our natural desire to belong, collaborate, feel authentically seen and heard, and create a positive impact on others.

With larger companies, creating win-win relationships and developing community from those win-wins make other traffic channels work better. With smaller businesses, win-win relationships are the best marketing strategy you can deploy. I recommend making them your primary focus until you have enough resources built up to engage in multichannel marketing.

THE SYNERGISTIC POWER OF THE WIN-WIN

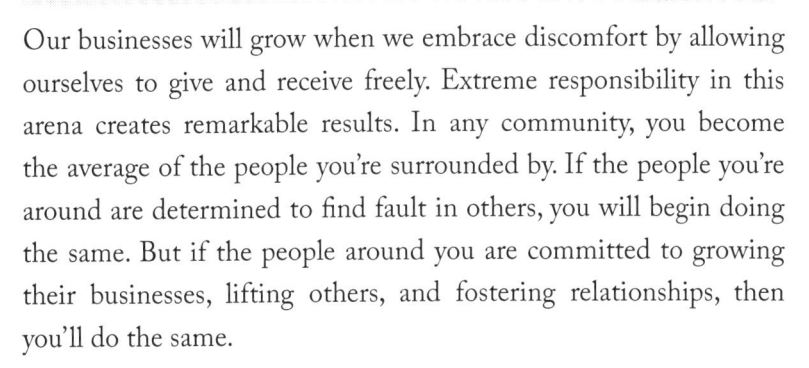

Our businesses will grow when we embrace discomfort by allowing ourselves to give and receive freely. Extreme responsibility in this arena creates remarkable results. In any community, you become the average of the people you're surrounded by. If the people you're around are determined to find fault in others, you will begin doing the same. But if the people around you are committed to growing their businesses, lifting others, and fostering relationships, then you'll do the same.

In her 2015 bestseller, *Rising Strong*, Brene Brown shares the philosophy of assuming positive intent: "What is the fundamental belief underpinning the assumption of positive intent? That people are doing the best they can."[5] She also writes, "All I know is that my life is better when I assume that people are doing their best. It keeps me out of judgment and lets me focus on what is, and not what should or could be."[5]

When you look around, are you investing your life, business, and time in people you want to be like? Do you want to talk like they talk? Do you want to create companies like the ones they have? Do you want to have relationships like the ones they have? Do they have trouble getting new clients, or do they have a waiting list? Are they constantly at odds with others? Are their relationships with their clients positive and a constant source of referrals?

I encourage you to surround yourself with people who see the good in everyone because there is so much opportunity when we know where to focus. In deciding whether you're investing in the right people, ask yourself the following:

- Am I part of a positive movement?
- Do I feel connected to a greater solution offered to the world?
- When I share with others, are they affirming and optimistic about what's possible?
- Do the people I'm surrounded by believe that everyone is doing their best?

If you're anchored to people who drag others down, it might be time to find a new community or create your own community where you can serve at a higher level. Although leaving one community behind and shifting to a new one is uncomfortable, when you take that leap; there's a beautiful, synergistic effect. When you build visibility, credibility, and community, it generates collaborations and referrals that grow your business.

A WINNING FORMULA

At this point, you might be wondering "This is all great, Laura, but how do I develop referrals, find more collaborators, and grow an audience of qualified leads?" The win-win formula illustrates how you can combine the strategies outlined in this book to generate new business over time. The key phrase is *over time*.

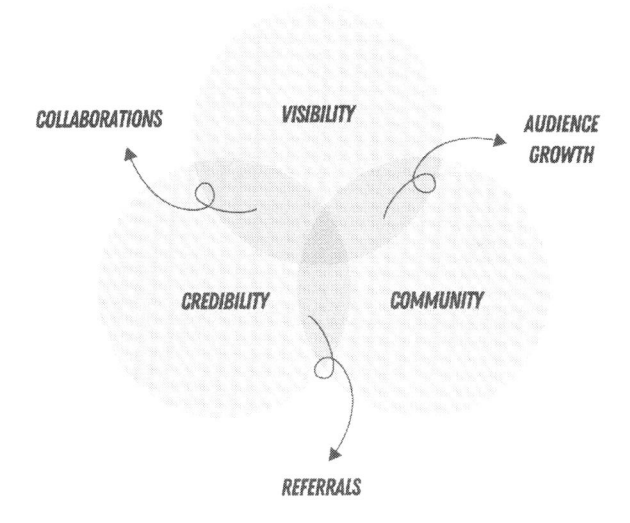

Win-Win
FORMULA

COLLABORATIONS VISIBILITY AUDIENCE GROWTH

CREDIBILITY COMMUNITY

REFERRALS

The win-win formula doesn't produce results overnight, but building relationships creates long-term, sustainable growth. Most entrepreneurs underestimate what can happen in a decade but overestimate what can happen in a year. If you plan on being in business for a long time, start playing the long game by engaging in regular collaborations and increasing your visibility, credibility, and community. It might feel uncomfortable initially, but as it becomes part of your routine, collaborations, new audience members, and referrals will flow in.

Going back to my love of tennis, I played tennis competitively in high school and college and was a top-rated player. After my schooling was over, career and family took priority, and my tennis game was relegated to an occasional (as in every few years) hitting session with my dad. A year after my third child was born and about 18 months into the pandemic, I realized that I needed to get out of my house regularly to maintain my sanity.

"Tennis!" I thought. "Perfect solution. It takes place outside with limited contact and much socialization. What could be a better mid-pandemic sport? Plus, I'm good at tennis (or at least I used to be). I'll join a local tennis club and start playing again."

When I went out to play for the first time, I quickly realized that I was nowhere near as good as I used to be and that getting my groove back wouldn't be easy. When I tried to play competitively, I was embarrassingly turned down for an intermediate team. I started to get discouraged. It was frustrating. I wanted to be an advanced player immediately, just like I used to be. Three kids and 20 years shouldn't make that big of a difference, right?

Each time I wanted to give up, I took up a new mantra: "This is going to take time."

When I saw people playing in a group I'd been excluded from, I'd say, "It's just going to take time."

When I lost a match, I felt I should have won, I'd say, "This will improve over time."

I must have repeated some version of this mantra to myself a hundred times over the last year. I'm not back to my former level of play yet, but I'm confident I'll be an advanced player again in the next few years.

The thoughts we choose about long-term work have much to do with our ability to see things through to the point of finding success. For most things worth doing, we can't expect to reap a harvest on the same day we plant the seed. The development of continual win-wins that add up to consistent audience growth, collaborations, and referrals takes time. With each partnership, interaction, and relationship, we build relational capital that cultivates additional win-wins in our businesses. Over time, just like with my tennis game, your business will grow beyond recognition; you'll be an advanced player in business because of all the small win-wins adding up.

As credibility drives collaborations with suitable types of business owners and you build visibility in the marketplace, you'll attract higher caliber peers.

Collaborations have a multiplier effect on your business. You spend less time speaking to the wrong type of clients and find yourself in front of your ideal audience. This kind of audience is not particularly price sensitive or untrusting because they're hearing your unique perspective in your own words, which creates a genuine connection that increases the overall value of your services.

And as your visibility within a community grows, the audience of people you give to expands, contributing to the overall goodwill toward your business. A hundred true fans extend into 200, 500, and ultimately, to the ideal of 1,000 or more. These true fans are members of your audience, podcast listeners, blog and book readers, and superfans—those who love what you do and are happy to share it with anyone who will listen.

When you have credibility within a community, the mere exposure effect kicks in, and referrals stream in, just like they did in my $70,000 webinar story. Referrals come to me every week not because I asked for them, but because of the trust others place in me and the connections I've developed with them.

The win-win formula is the simplest growth strategy.

Show up and make yourself visible through strategic collaborations.

Consistently demonstrate credibility by creating value for others.

Over time, this builds trust and generates referrals and introductions.

This simple formula has been around since the inception of a market economy for a reason—it works.

COMPLEMENTARY BUSINESSES: THE RIGHT FORMULA FOR COLLABORATION

Natalie and I met through mutual friends while networking in a community together. We immediately saw the value in each other's services. Physical wellness—Natalie's specialty— is not an area I work in, but it's a powerful tool for transformation and health. Natalie teaches women how to physically embrace their power and strength, and I teach the same thing in an emotional, energetic way. Because our services are complimentary, we realized that if we collaborated, we could enhance our service to our clients. So we decided to try a platform exchange. I asked Natalie to do an Instagram Live post on my channel and encouraged my clients to get in touch with her. Afterward, Natalie invited me to speak in her community. After that first platform exchange, we started swapping services. Now, we use each other's services, collaborate on social media, and support and refer each other. We have received referrals from our collaborative connection as we continue to work together. To me, the win-win is in how our complementary businesses help us serve our clientele and in the expansion of our followings that has resulted from our collaboration.

—Jennifer Olson, Laughing Lotus Wellness

Focus on showing up at a high level and give your all. The point is to connect; that provides purpose and meaning to our lives. Find connections. Build relationships. Develop bridges for others. This kind of generosity and intentionality will enrich your life and catapult your business to extraordinary new heights.

LANDING DREAM COLLABORATORS

The late Chet Holmes developed a sales strategy called the Dream 100, a method that helps people find dream clients. According to Chet Holmes International, the Dream 100 strategy was invented when Chet worked for billionaire Charlie Munger, one of today's most celebrated investors.

Charlie trusted Chet to take his small newspaper at the time and put it on the map and Chet was provided a database of 2200 advertisers. His job was to make hundreds of cold calls daily and try to win their business.

After much frustration from a lack of progress, he started an analysis and found that only 167 companies purchased 95 percent of the market.

As result, Chet sent 167 of the best buyers direct mail every two weeks, followed by a call twice a month. Since these were already the biggest buyers, the first four months of intensive marketing and selling brought no actual reward. In the fifth month, Chet Holmes closed his first deal—Xerox. The biggest deal that the industry had ever seen was a 15-page full-color spread. He closed 28 more of his dream buyers for the next five months, and history was born. Within only 12 to 15 months of implementing his unique methodologies, Chet managed to double the sales volume of the nine divisions he was running for Munger.[6]

By focusing on a small, specific population of his ideal clients, Chet could generate some of the most significant orders in the company's history. The takeaway from this story is that your dream clients will be few in number but will provide the bulk of your revenue. When it comes to developing a win-win relationship, your dream 100 are your top 100 clients and collaborators.

The dream 100 strategy includes drafting a good profile of your best niche buyers and potential collaborators. Then create a list of who they are among your contacts or your contact's contacts and reach out to them regularly. Use social media and your connections to gain visibility with this specific audience. This marketing plan is affordable, systematic, and repeatable, regardless of your industry.

You can use the content you're already creating—social media posts, emails, articles, and podcasts—to build connections with your dream 100 lists. If you see on LinkedIn or elsewhere that you have connections in common, take advantage of that. Every interaction with your dream 100 develops credibility because familiarity breeds trust. Keep in mind that finding your dream 100 is a long-term strategy. Have patience as you build visibility and trust with this select group of contacts. You *will* see results.

Years ago, I made a list of my own dream 100 clients and collaborators, and at the time many individuals on that list were unfamiliar with my work. Today they are familiar with my work because I purposely increased my proximity to them until they couldn't help but take notice. Some of them have since become clients and partners.

CHAPTER SUMMARY

The last step in developing win-win relationships is ensuring you're part of a community that shares your values and beliefs. There is a multitude of benefits to such a community. In community, we're never alone and never short of encouragement or advice. We're kept off the sidelines, engaged, and active. We share our experiences and learn from how others have navigated the situations we're facing. Your business will prosper when growing credibility and visibility are coupled with community. That's the magic of the win-win formula.

CHAPTER 7

DON'T FEAR THE WIN-LOSE

Throughout this book we've been discussing developing win-win collaborations, and I'm sure you're eager to start making connections and creating reciprocal exchanges. But many of us have been burned by bad experiences in the past. When a win-win exchange goes south, I call it a win-lose. As you work on developing win-wins, don't fear the win-lose. Not every collaboration will work out but don't let that stop you from creating win-wins in the future.

THE FUTURE IS COLLABORATION— BUT EXPERIENCE MAKES US THINK TWICE ABOUT IT

The future of business growth is open collaboration. In entrepreneurship, it is mission critical to find like-minded, big-picture thinkers with whom we can create, collaborate, partner, and lead. In a business context that includes changing social media algorithms, rising advertising costs, and pandemic-induced uncertainty. The one thing you can consistently rely on is the people you've built connections with inside your network.

The problem is that, although we all want to develop community and collaborations, business culture hasn't always been conducive to either one. Many of us have experienced disappointments and betrayals. We've gone through hurtful situations involving people we would've loved collaborating with.

Women supporting women sounds great in an Instagram or Pinterest quote, but the practical application of it is challenging. We all have a story that goes like this:

"Wow, I thought this person had my back, but they clearly did not."

That sting and discomfort has happened to all of us. When we're on the receiving end of someone else's scarcity thinking, it makes us want to withdraw. It makes us want to say, "Forget it. I'm going to do this on my own. I don't need anyone else."

Yet, the pain of past negative experiences sometimes blocks our ability to be open and welcoming; these experiences may even keep us from making the positive impact for which we were created. We must reverse course and be available to potential collaborators in doing meaningful work and contributing to the greater good in the world. Be encouraged that reciprocity is part of the human condition. Often, you'll do something nice for someone out of generosity, and it'll come back to you when you least expect it. The favor might not be returned the next day or week, but it will be returned at some point. Many of us are very generous. We're givers, and that's why we became entrepreneurs, right? But we tend to go solo on the entrepreneurial journey, and when someone reaches out to us, we dismiss the connection. We say, "Oh no, thank you. I don't need that." We must allow ourselves to receive outreach, generosity, and care to accept the gift of reciprocity when it shows up.

It's the easiest thing in the world to say, "I'm going to give without expectation of receiving something in return. I will enjoy the pure energetic abundance of doing something for someone else." The human brain is wired for this kind of generosity. If you're thinking, "Oh, I would love for people to pop up in my inbox, offering to help me with the growth of my company," there's a way to create that: give without expectation of receiving anything in return. The moment we shift our energy toward giving, everything around us also shifts. Opportunities and connections that wouldn't otherwise have been available start showing up. As you grow your business and brand and create financial success and security in your business and personal life, you'll become confident that creating win-win partnerships will fuel your company's growth. You'll be less worried about the next sale and more focused on making a difference. Look for meaningful relationships that don't feel like transactions. Aim to work for the pure joy of knowing you're making a positive impact.

A SUPPORTIVE COLLABORATION

I met Jennifer Major through a mutual friend, and we immediately saw the value in each other's services. Because people struggle to organize fitness and food prep in their busy lives, Jennifer's organizational business helps my clients prioritize health. We are passionate about how our services can impact our clients' lives and have begun to collaborate on social media together with live video. As we continue to support one another's communities, Jennifer works with me on my time management, and I now refer many people to her who need help to get organized with their time and schedule. She also invites me to participate in live videos on her Instagram and in her group, where I receive dozens of referrals. We continue to work together and support each other with engagement on social, accountability each week, and business growth.

—Natalie Hurley, NH Personal Training

We may use all kinds of excuses not to initiate these kinds of exchanges and with just cause. I can share a horror story from my business experience that would make you say, "Oh my gosh! I'm surprised you ever left the house again." But it's not essential to be right about the risks of being an entrepreneur who positively impacts the world. What's important is supporting other people and allowing yourself to be supported so that you can benefit from the beauty of reciprocity. If I had allowed myself to withdraw because of being burned in the past, I would never have found the fantastic win-win partnerships I have in my business. New opportunities appear when we approach business with the conviction of limitless possibilities.

BEING ON THE OUTSIDE OF A COMMUNITY

Embracing community is one of the most beautiful avenues to take, professionally and personally. It might take a while to find your people, and that's okay, but keep going and keep making connections. Continue to pursue connections and know that only good can come from those relationships.

When you join a community, don't paralyze yourself with questions:

- Do they like me?
- What if I'm not good enough?
- Am I accepted here?
- Is this safe for me?

These kinds of questions come from past experiences; they make us stay small and remain where we're comfortable. Be empowered! No matter what hardship you've endured, you can be intentional about putting yourself back out there.

As you enter into a new community, ask yourself the following:

- What do we have in common?
- How can I show up in this community and be a contributor?
- How can we connect or collaborate based on the things we share in common?"

Remember, we steer where we stare. If, based on your past experiences, you're looking to prove to yourself (even subconsciously) that a new group of people isn't safe, you'll miss out on the blessings that come with abundance and reciprocity.

We all pass through rough seasons in business. We sometimes experience challenging circumstances at home. You may not show up as your best self when you're going through something. You might show up in ways that don't reflect your core beliefs. But I'd like to challenge you to show up as a giver, a helper, a person that invests first, then your experience will be completely different.

Esther Inman, a colleague I met in a mastermind, teaches thousands of people each year how to work from home as virtual assistants (VAs) with her signature program, 90 Day VA. She had a critical team member, Deya Aliaga, who made everything in her business run like clockwork. When Deya told Esther that she wanted to leave to focus on a business idea of her own, Esther was initially disappointed. But her desire to see others succeed in their dreams and goals was more important than keeping Deya on at 90 Day VA. Esther says, "There was definitely a grieving period, where I was sad about the relationship ending in its current form, particularly because our dynamic together was so magical. And at the same time, I was happy for her because I knew that she has so much to offer the world and would be outstanding at this next phase in her career."[2]

Esther parted with Deya as an employee and supported her by becoming a joint-venture partner for Deya's new business, which resulted in commissions of over $100,000 back to Esther's business. Because of her history with Deya, Esther knew that if she referred her students to Deya, they would be incredibly well taken care of, so she enthusiastically sent them Deya's way. A situation that Esther could have viewed as a win-lose was transformed into a powerful win-win by a simple shift in perspective.

My own story is not without intense relational hardships. When we present ourselves to the world by starting a business, we attract like-minded souls who are ideal audience members, customers, and collaborators. But we can also trigger negativity in others. I once had a competitor pretending to be a customer, posting mean comments on my blog, and creating fake bad reviews online. I was sued and forced into bankruptcy by a group of former partners and competitors, only to have the case dismissed years later, once the damage was done. Win-wins are easy to think about when things are copacetic; they're harder to stay committed to when we're tempted to match someone else's fear-based decisions. Matching fear with fear will spiral into continual lose-lose situations.

Despite the challenges I've faced, I believe that God created every one of us with unique skills, abilities, and talents. Everyone has something brilliant to contribute to the world. When I see a lose-lose emerging, my question is, "What would love do?" Thinking this way always leads me to the correct answer. Sometimes it's to forgive; sometimes it's to set proper boundaries; and sometimes it's to bless and release. Our dreams are tested when we run into disagreements or challenges with others. But we must operate from the belief that everyone has value to foster win-wins. We don't have to agree with everyone, but we need to value diverse opinions and ideas so that we can learn and broaden our perspectives. We need to have enough humility to understand that no one knows everything and that we can learn from *all* experiences. When we hold this perspective, a situation that initially feels like a win-lose may transform into a win-win.

For many people, the collective trauma of the pandemic and the upheaval we've experienced is an excellent reason to duck for cover. It's normal to feel that way, even for the most extroverted among us (I like to say that I put the *extra* in extrovert). Instead, I think we

> *A situation that initially feels like a win-lose may transform itself into a win-win.*
>
> — Laura Meyer

should embrace the feeling of vulnerability and understand that it's something everyone is experiencing. Don't let negative experiences discourage you to the point where you go it alone. Over time, you'll learn to see the signs of a win-lose forming. You'll learn to recognize when it's time to cut your losses, set clearer boundaries, and know when to open yourself up to new possibilities. One of the great benefits of free will is that we choose the story we want to live in. Do you want to live in a story of sadness and defeat or one of possibility? As entrepreneurs, we're faced with this choice every day. No one can write the script for us. Take ownership of your story.

DEALING WITH NEGATIVITY

The more you grow, the more significant your influence and the more likely you'll encounter upheavals, challenges, and negativity. It's going to happen. There will come a day when people assume things about you that are entirely wrong. It's okay. Let them be wrong about you. You can't please everyone, whether they're part of your audience or part of someone else's audience. Instead, stand by your values, have a positive approach, and be confident. Think of anyone you respect and look up to. I guarantee they have people who disapprove of them. It's a normal thing to experience. Ultimately, being an example of light and love is a matchless way to contribute to more good in the world. Don't allow yourself to be brought down by the challenges you face; instead, make the commitment to continual win-wins.

DO IT ANYWAY

People are often unreasonable, irrational, and self-centered. Forgive them anyway.

If you are kind, people may accuse you of selfish, ulterior motives. Be kind anyway.

If you are successful, you will win some unfaithful friends and some genuine enemies.

Succeed anyway.

If you are honest and sincere people may deceive you. Be honest and sincere anyway.

What you spend years creating, others could destroy overnight. Create anyway.

If you find serenity and happiness, some may be jealous. Be happy anyway.

The good you do today, will often be forgotten. Do good anyway.

Give the best you have, and it will never be enough. Give your best anyway.

In the final analysis, it is between you and God. It was never between you and them anyway.

—Mother Teresa[3]

CHAPTER SUMMARY

Not every collaboration will work out. We know from challenging personal experiences that many things can go wrong in professional relationships, but we shouldn't let our past hold us back from being open to collaboration. It's in our human nature to give to others; that part is relatively easy. But we also need to be available to receive help from others. When we're in relationships where we both give and receive, we're open to possibility, and we've entered into the beautiful abundance and reciprocity of the win-win.

Common Questions

Is there a particular platform that is better than others for collaborations?
I don't believe that any single platform is better than all the others. But I think you have to commit to one platform you feel good about and enjoy it. If, for example, you love writing and hate being on video, don't choose Instagram reels as your primary platform. You're not going to last very long on that platform. There are a lot of great platforms that you can be a part of. It's entirely legitimate for somebody with a Facebook group to be on your LinkedIn Live and for you, if your primary platform is LinkedIn, to guest on their Facebook group. It's more important to have a highly engaged audience that trusts you than to be on a specific platform or a platform of a certain size.

What should I do if someone wants me to feature them in my podcast, but they're not offering to do anything for me in return?
There may be situations where you feature others because you like their content, which would be valuable to your audience, and you don't feel that a two-way exchange is necessary. But if that isn't the case, you can respond by asking, "Do you have a platform on which you can feature me?" If the answer is no, simply reply, "I'm saving the limited spots on my podcast for reciprocal exchanges because I'm also looking to increase my visibility. I'd love to have you on my podcast at some point, so when you get your platform up and running, please let me know, and we can schedule a time for us to be on each other's shows."

I am constantly being pitched to get on connection calls, which overloads my calendar. What should I do?

How often have you been pitched for connection chats in your LinkedIn inbox? I've seen many business owners reluctantly agree to such meetings only to burn out and give up on relationship marketing altogether. It's common to either allow yourself to get entirely overwhelmed by scheduling too many calls or shut down all potential meetings because you see them as a waste of time.

Connection calls can be beneficial but not relevant unless you're purposeful in taking them. Here's how to get the most out of them.

First, take time to connect with people who interest you, who excite you, who energize you—those you'd like as a friend and those who've established credibility with you through group activities or events. To make the most out of connection calls, your connections need to have the potential to fall into one of the following four categories:

1. Collaboration partners
2. Referral partners
3. Clients
4. Friends

If they don't fall into one of these four categories, it's probably better to politely decline. If you realize that a call might turn into a pitch, you could redirect to an event you'll be attending. For example, you might say, "I don't have time for a call this week, but let's connect at this free event I'll be attending on Thursday." This allows you to scope the person out in a larger group setting before getting on a call with them.

The mistake that many people make is to automatically assume that they should get on a connection call with everyone who asks. It's best to schedule calls with people you've connected with in a group setting, such as an event or a program you're both part of. That way, you can ensure that a connection call isn't going to turn into a direct-sales opportunity, which can make you feel like you never want to hear the words "connection" or "call" ever again.

When it comes to connection calls, pace yourself. Prioritize events and organizations where you can get a feel for people in a group setting before spending time with them one-on-one. When it comes to outreach, be thoughtful about whom you reach out to by knowing why it makes sense for you to connect on both sides and explain why it could be a win-win.

Aim to only have connection calls at times that work well for your schedule, so you don't get overwhelmed or infringe on time you've set aside for other priorities. When you commit to showing up, make sure you show up. If you have to cancel on short notice, it's helpful to explain what happened as a courtesy—"My child is sick," or "I have a client who is having a tough time and needs to speak with me." It's essential to be very gracious if you cancel. If you have to cancel, do so with at least a 48-hour notice. If you don't show up, don't expect the person to reschedule; you wasted their time, and they have every right to say, "No, thank you." If someone doesn't show up for you, it is your prerogative to say, "I cannot reschedule."

Where can I get some of the resources and templates you mention in this book?
Glad you asked! Visit createyourwinwin.com to download easy-to-use free tools to enjoy and be inspired by as you create win-win relationships in your business. On the same website, I'll be answering additional questions as they come in from readers of this book.

Thank you FOR READING my book

I value your perspective and appreciate what you have to say.

Please take a few minutes to leave a helpful review on Amazon and also let me know what you thought of the book.

Thank you so much!

With gratitude,

Laura Meyer

Acknowledgements

The world is a better place because of those who want to build genuine relationships with others. To all the companies I've had the opportunity to consult with and coach, thank you for being the inspiration for *Win-Win*.

Leading an exceptional team is a true honor. Without support from my dream team at JoyBrand Creative, this book would never have been written. To my business support system, mentors, prayer partners, friends, past and present partners, and business besties, you've given me the love and confidence to keep going and provided me with the guidance that I needed in order to see my blind spots and balance out my strengths. Thank you to Shana, Ciara, Beka, Jennifer, Emily, Lindsay, Julie, Stan, Lauren, Aryeh, Natalie, Stephen, Kelly, Carrie, Heidi, and my parents, Dave and Debbie.

Writing a book is a massive undertaking that requires a big commitment from all parties. Tremendous thanks to my publishing team at Happy Self-Publishing for making *Win-Win* a reality, and a special thank you Calligraphy by Josie Lyn at Phinley Design Co. for your beautiful handiwork found throughout this book.

And most of all, I want to thank God and His grace, His wonderful enabling grace. Thank you for helping me get through the most difficult hardships in my life with a spirit of peace and forgiveness. Ephesians 2:7 NIV says, "In order that in the coming ages he might show the incomparable riches of his grace, expressed in his kindness to us in Christ Jesus."

I am beyond grateful that God has chosen to use the ashes of where I've been to create beauty for others.

Take Your Business to the Next Level

FREE RESOURCES

Download the following free resources at www.createyourwinwin.com to help your business grow.

FREE Build your authority online with a core message: Download 37 templates that help you stand out and become visible. Begin to attract clients by building your authority online.

FREE Niching templates: Get three messaging templates you can try out as you niche down (and level up!) whom you serve in the marketplace.

FREE Social media story collaboration campaign: Begin to create collaboration exchanges with easy-to-use templates.

FREE Introduction scripts: Want to introduce two fantastic people to one another? Met someone awesome but not sure how to follow up? Visit createyourwinwin.com and get my introduction scripts. They'll give you the exact words you need to follow up with your most recent connection!

Ways to Work With Laura

Fractional Freedom Consulting Incubator—apply to be in the next cohort!

If you love business growth and want to make strategy your thing, look at my Fractional Freedom Consulting Incubator, which opens for enrollment several times a year.

You can find out more about the next cohort at www.getfractionalfreedom.com.

JoyBrand Creative

If you're an established business owner looking for hands-on growth advice, you can apply to work with my team and me directly at www.scalewithjoy.com.

I'd love to hear from you!

Subscribe to my podcast: Next Level Leap

FOLLOW ME ON SOCIAL MEDIA AT

www.linkedin.com/in/laura-meyer-creative/
www.instagram.com/lauraemeyer/
www.facebook.com/laurameyerconsulting

Permissions

We acknowledge the following individuals for granting permission to share their stories and be cited in the book.

Jennifer Allwood, Author + Influencer | jenniferallwood.com

Patty Palmer, Deep Space Sparkle | www.deepspacesparkle.com

Gino Wickman and Rob Dube, The 10 Disciplines | www.the10disciplines.com

Esther Inman, 90 Day VA | www.90dayva.com

Ali Brown, The Trust | alibrown.com

Tresa Todd, The Women's Real Estate Investment Network | womensrein.com

Tanya Dalton, Best-Selling Author | tanyadalton.com

Aryeh Sheinbein, Business Consultant & Strategist | insidethelionsdenpodcast.com

Martha Cristina Garza, Branding Strategist | marthacgarza.com

Julia Taylor, CEO & Founder of GeekPack | geekpack.com

Jena Castro-Casbon, MS-CCC SLP | independentclinician.com

Anna Phillips, Founder of The Lash Lounge | www.thelashlounge.com

Shana Lynn Bresnahan, Community Strategist | www.shanalynn.com

Kris Plachy, Leadership is Feminine | krisplachy.com

Notes

INTRODUCTION

1. Annemarie Kelleghan, "The Social Media Disconnect," *Psychology Today* (blog), February 26, 2018, https://www.psychologytoday.com/us/blog/home-base/201802/the-socialmedia-disconnect.

2. Thomas G. Bognanno, "Digitally Disconnected: When Social Media Doesn't Feel Social," *Thrive* (blog), *Thrive Global*, undated, https://thriveglobal.com/stories/digitallydisconnected-when-social-media-doesnt-feel-social/.

CHAPTER 1

1. Sarah Frier, "Facebook's AI Mistakenly Bans Ads for Struggling Businesses," *Bloomberg Quint* (blog), *Bloomberg*, November 27, 2020, https://www.bqprime.com/business/facebook-s-ai-mistakenly-bans-ads-for-strugglingbusinesses.

2. Kevin Kelly, "1000 True Fans," *The Technium* (blog), March 4, 2008, https://kk.org/thetechnium/1000-true-fans/.

CHAPTER 2

1. Drew Calvert, "Cultivating Trust Is Critical—and Surprisingly Complex," *Kellogg Insight* (blog), March 7, 2016, https://insight.kellogg.northwestern.edu/article/cultivating-trust-iscritical-and-surprisingly-complex.

2. Kent Grayson, "3 Components of Trust in Buyer-Seller Relationships: A Marketer's Perspective," produced by The Trust Project at Northwestern University, accessed on April 7, 2022, video, https://www.kellogg.northwestern.edu/trust-project/videos/graysonep-1.aspx.

3. Christine Alemany, "3 Ways Marketers Can Earn—and Keep—Customer Trust," *Harvard Business Review* (blog), June 3, 2022, https://hbr.org/2022/06/3-ways-marketers-canearn-and-keep-customer-trust.

4. Tresa Todd, personal communication to the author, August 15, 2022

CHAPTER 3

1. Adam Grant, *Give and Take* (London: Penguin, 2013).

2. Adam Grant, "Are You a Giver or a Taker?" produced by TED, published on January 24, 2017, YouTube video, https://www.youtube.com/watch?v=YyXRYgjQXX0.

3. Charlotte Nickerson, "What Is the Mere Exposure Effect?" *Simply Psychology* (blog), March 8, 2022, https://www.simplypsychology.org/mere-exposure-effect.html.

CHAPTER 4

1. Koba Molenaar, "20 Podcast Statistics You Should Know in 2022," *Influencer Marketing Hub* (blog), updated May 3, 2022, https://influencermarketinghub.com/podcast-statistics/.

2. Margy Feldhuhn, personal communication to the author, August 10, 2022

3. Napoleon Hill, *The Think and Grow Rich Action Pack* (New York: Plume, 1990).

4. "About Us," Dress for Success, accessed August 23, 2022, https://dressforsuccess.org/about-us/.

5. Stephanie Burns, "Affiliate Partnerships: Why You Should Consider Them and How to Get Started," *ForbesWomen* (blog), *Forbes*, September 1, 2020, https://www.forbes.com/sites/stephanieburns/2020/09/01/affiliate-partnerships-why-youshould-consider-them-and-how-to-get-started/.

CHAPTER 5

1. Dan Ariely, "Ask Ariely: On Gifting Gratitude and Requesting Reply," *Ask Ariely* (blog), November 20, 2021, https://danariely.com/8120-2/.

CHAPTER 6

1. "Future of Health Care Is Creating Environmental Change," Blue Zones, accessed on August 23, 2022, https://www.bluezones.com/2018/08/future-of-health-care-is-creatingenvironmental-change/.

2. Fergal Glynn, "Why It Takes 6-8 Marketing Touches to Generate a Viable Sales Lead," *The 360 Blog* (blog), *SalesForce*, April 16, 2015, https://www.salesforce.com/blog/takes6-8-touches-generate-viable-sales-lead-heres-why-gp/.

3. The Trust, accessed August 23, 2022, https://jointhetrust.org/.

4. "About," Ali Brown, accessed August 23, 2022, https://alibrown.com/about/.

5. Brene Brown, *Rising Strong* (New York: Spiegel & Grau, 2015).

6. Eric H., "The Story of the Dream 100 Strategy," *Chet Holmes International* (blog), February 12, 2021, https://chetholmes.com/the-story-of-the-dream-100-strategy/.

CHAPTER 7

1. Jon Sundt, "Why Entrepreneurs Are the Happiest Givers," *HuffPost* (blog), December 18, 2013, https://www.huffpost.com/entry/why-entrepreneurs-are-the_b_4460134.

2. Esther Inman, personal communication with the author, August 8, 2022.

3. Mother Teresa, "St. Teresa of Calcutta (Mother Teresa): Do It Anyway," *Features* (blog), *PrayerFoundation Evangelical Lay Monks*, undated, https://prayerfoundation.net/stteresa-of-calcutta-mother-teresa-do-it-anyway/.

About the Author

LAURA MEYER is a growth marketing consultant and powerhouse connector. As a serial entrepreneur who has scaled multiple six- and seven-figure online and offline companies over the last 20 years, Laura knows firsthand the power of relationships and their importance to business growth.

Several years ago, Laura made the difficult decision to close her traditional business without any idea what she would do next. Because of her network and relationships, she would reemerge as an expert among experts, a strategic marketing consultant, and a fractional chief marketing officer to some of the country's top influencers. In addition, she co-founded the Advance Women's Expert Network with Kelly Roach, helping hundreds of women worldwide develop powerful expert brands through community, connection, and collaboration with others who share their values and spirit. Her highly acclaimed podcast, the Next Level Leap, has had over 30,000 downloads, and her consulting certification program, Fractional Freedom, has helped dozens of smart experts become in-demand consultants.

Outside of work, you can find Laura soaking in family time with her family of five in southeast Pennsylvania. In her spare time, Laura attempts to relive her high school years playing tennis, and when no one else is home (which is rare!), she kicks up her feet to binge-watch HGTV.

To find out more about working with Laura and her team or to inquire about Laura's availability as a speaker, you can contact her at www.joybrandcreative.com.

Printed in Great Britain
by Amazon